# TO THE *Purchaser*
## of this Book, from its Publisher:—

ALL PAPER, *including the paper on which books are printed, as well as the materials which go into the manufacture of paper, is absolutely essential to the prosecution of the war.*

§§ Because of this, book publishers are now seriously restricted in the amount of paper which is available for books. For 1944 my firm is allowed but three-quarters as many pounds of paper as we used in the calendar year of 1942.

§§ This means that unless we economize in the use of paper in every way possible, we shall not be able to print anything like all of the books readers will demand of us. This is particularly important because our list abounds in good books published as long as twenty years ago (the Borzoi was founded in 1915) for which there is still steady demand and which we do not wish to let go out of print.

§§ We are therefore reducing the size of our books and also their thickness, and have made an effort, without sacrificing readability, to reduce the number of pages by getting more printed-matter on each page. For this we must beg your indulgence, though I think that in many ways the smaller and thinner books are more attractive to handle and to read than their larger and fatter fellows. On the other hand, despite the shortage of all materials that go into the making of books and the critical manpower shortage among all printers and binders, we intend in every way possible to preserve those physical qualities which have long made Borzoi Books outstanding. We will use cloths of as good quality as we can procure and will maintain the same high standards of typographical and binding design.

# André Gide

Strait Is the Gate (1924)

Dostoevsky (1926)
*with an Introduction by Arnold Bennett*

Lafcadio's Adventures (1927)
*(first published under the title*
The Vatican Swindle, *1925)*

The Counterfeiters (1927)

Travels in the Congo (1929)

The School for Wives (1929)

The Immoralist (1930)

Two Symphonies (1931)
*Isabelle · The Pastoral Symphony*

Return from the U.S.S.R. (1937)

*These are* Borzoi Books, *published by*
Alfred · A · Knopf

# IMAGINARY INTERVIEWS

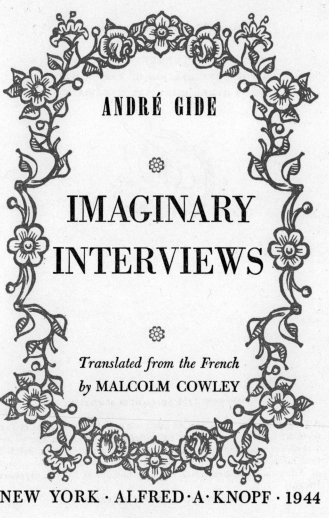

ANDRÉ GIDE

✳

# IMAGINARY
# INTERVIEWS

✳

*Translated from the French*
*by* MALCOLM COWLEY

NEW YORK · ALFRED·A·KNOPF · 1944

**le, André Paul Guillaume.** Imaginary
erviews; tr. from the French by Mal-
m Cowley. 1944. 172p. Knopf, $2.

st of these essays on literary subjects are
dialog form and are therefore called inter-
ws. They originally appeared in the liter-
supplement of *Le Figaro*, published in the
ee zone of France, during 1941 and 1942,
d while they are strictly on literary sub-
ts, such as the form of French verse, the
nslator points out that anti-Nazi sentiments
n be read into them. Scholarly; limited ap-
al.

3.91  French literature—Hist. & crit.    44-8537

they represent the reactions to France's tra-


( continued on back flap )

( *continued from front flap* )

vail, to problems of intense urgency, on the part of one of the most complex and colorful minds of our time.

Gide adopted the form of the imaginary interview as a method of getting into French newspapers things that could not otherwise have been printed there after June 1940. This fact explains why several of the interviews turn out, on careful reading, not to be dealing with their purported subject matter, but with far wider issues. To these interviews several other of Gide's recent writings have been joined. One of them is an introduction to the theater of Goethe. Another, already renowned throughout the French-speaking world, is Gide's philosophic attack on Marc Chardonne, the first important French writer to advocate collaboration with the Nazis. Still another, and by no means the least moving, is Gide's firsthand report of the liberation of Tunis, where he now resides.

Translating so careful and subtle a writer as Gide is a difficult task. It has been expertly performed by Malcolm Cowley, whose introduction and notes add immeasurably to the value of this book for English-speaking readers.

# CONTENTS

# INTRODUCTION

THIS is not the place for a discussion of André Gide's career as a writer. We know already, or can easily learn, that he was born in Paris in 1869; that he was the only child of a rich Huguenot family; that his father died when André was eleven, leaving him in charge of a pious and possessive mother; that his boyhood friend was Pierre Louÿs, who was already writing hymns to Aphrodite; that he was one of the young Symbolist poets invited to Mallarmé's Tuesday evenings (others were Jules Laforgue, Stefan George, Henri de Régnier, Francis Vielé-Griffin, Paul Valéry, and Paul Claudel, perhaps the most distinguished group of poets who in modern times have regarded themselves as the disciples of a single master); that he suffered from a conflict between Christianity and his pagan instincts, with the instincts victorious for the moment (but the struggle continued, for Christianity had become an instinct with him, too); that he became known as a persistent traveler, always on his way home from Bayreuth or Biskra; that for a long time his influence in French literature was extensive but almost subterranean, since most of his books were

printed in limited editions and soon went out of print;
that he was the guiding spirit of the group that founded
the *Nouvelle Revue Française*, which enjoyed more prestige among serious writers than any other magazine
published in Europe, and perhaps in the world; that he
caused a scandal by the publication of his alarmingly
frank autobiography, *If It Die;* that he became disillusioned about Communism as a result of his trip to Russia
in 1936, but didn't permit his disillusionment to color
his life or make him the enemy of every cause he suspected the Communists of supporting; that his published work consists of seventy-odd volumes and that it
has covered almost every literary field, since it includes
poems and prose poems, plays, criticism, general essays,
personal memoirs and travel diaries, tales, short novels
in the classical French manner and one long novel, *The
Counterfeiters*, that is among the greatest of our time;
not to mention the extraordinary *Journal* that has been
appearing at intervals for the last twenty years and is
destined, perhaps, to be his principal achievement.

All these facts are widely known, as are others that
help to explain his character as a writer. The people
who have influenced him are first of all his mother (and
some day I hope to read a long study of French mothers
and their role in the Symbolist movement); then his boyhood friend, Pierre Louÿs; then Mallarmé, who gave
him the example of a life completely devoted to literature; then Oscar Wilde, whom he met at a critical moment in Algiers; then his cousin Emmanuèle, with whom
he fell in love when he was twelve years old and whom
he married shortly after his mother's death, so that she

came to occupy the same pious and maternal position in his life. Among literary influences, the first was the Bible, which he used to carry always in his coat pocket. The others might be listed in antithetical pairs: Racine and Shakespeare, Flaubert and Whitman, Goethe and Dostoyevsky—classicists and romanticists, masters of form and masters or slaves of emotion, Latins, Teutons, and Slavs. He says of himself: "I am a creature of dialogue; everything within me struggles against and contradicts itself." Hating the half-truth, he tries to give both sides of his inner arguments and to end by revealing himself scrupulously; no other French writer is more burdened with scruples. By his Calvinist sense of duty, he suggests New England: there are times when he seems to stand somewhere between Henry Adams and Henry James. By his disciplined individualism and the breadth of his literary interests, he suggests Goethe; and there was nobody else in the period between two wars who came so close to recapturing the place that Goethe held.

But these facts and notions have been treated at length (and a little too awesomely, I think) in several books about Gide, including those by Léon-Pierre Quint and Klaus Mann, which are available in English. I don't intend to trespass on their territory. The present introduction is concerned only with the *Imaginary Interviews* and how they came to be written.

After the fall of France, Gide wrote nothing for several months except brief and often puzzled entries in his *Journal*. He suffered, like many French writers, from a sense of guilt that was caused by the defeat itself, rather than by any misdeeds of his own. In life, guilt and punishment are often reversed, just as in the trial scene at the end of *Alice in Wonderland*. "Let the jury consider their verdict," the King said. "No, no!" said the Queen. "Sentence first—verdict afterwards." And there is the story from Grimm's *Fairy Tales* that Gide retells in his seventh interview: Herr Korbes, coming home to his cottage after the day's work, is assailed by a cat, a duck, and a whole collection of inanimate objects; when he tries to escape, a cobblestone falls and crushes his head. The story ends: "Herr Korbes must have been a very wicked man." Many French writers had subconsciously reached the same conclusion about themselves, feeling that they must have failed in their duty and have written very wicked books, or their nation would not have been punished.

This somewhat masochistic state of mind helps to explain why the Nazis were able to gain a certain number of converts—though self-interest was also involved, and the feeling that Hitler would continue to rule Europe in any case, so why not make the best of it?—and later, having committed themselves, they found that it was too late for them to change. Yet there were fewer turncoats in the literary world than is commonly supposed. Among the writers of some standing who went over to the Germans (omitting the journalists like Henri Béraud and Clément Vautel, who had always worn a For Sale sign round their necks, and omitting the ancient mummies like Abel Bonnard and Henri Bordeaux), there were chiefly Louis-Ferdinand Céline, Jean Cocteau, Paul Morand, Henry de Montherlant, Jean Giono, and two writers who would play a part in Gide's wartime career: Pierre Drieu la Rochelle and Jacques Chardonne. It is a fairly impressive list, but not one that represents the best in French letters. Drieu la Rochelle, now violently fascist, became the new editor of the *Nouvelle Revue Française*, the magazine that Gide had founded. It had been revived in Paris after the armistice, and the Germans wanted to keep it going for reasons of prestige. As for Chardonne, he wrote the first French book that accepted the defeat as a judgment and Hitler's triumph as a promise for the future. Gide read it and, for the first time since June 1940, he felt moved to take a public stand.

He discovered that honest political judgments could be printed even in Vichy France, so long as they were presented in the guise of literary criticism. Chardonne could not be attacked for his betrayal of French interests or his servility to the Germans; the censor would act immediately, not to mention the state police. But Chardonne could be condemned for vagueness, for affectation, for all sorts of literary faults that implied what Gide could not say about his political faults, and the censor could do nothing; perhaps in his heart he approved of the attack. "Chardonne plays for me," Gide said in the review he wrote for *Le Figaro*, which is reprinted at the end of this volume, "the part of the drunken helot, warning me against the wine for which I too might have shown a weakness. Seeing him reel and stagger, at once I stand erect." And he concluded: "Thanks to his fluidity and inconsistency (if I judge by myself), we have a better sense of our own steadfastness and, thanks to all these indistinct surrenders, of our own constancy." Gide was speaking not only for himself but for all the French writers who had so far been silent.

In November 1941 he began contributing a column to the literary supplement of *Le Figaro*, which was the best and almost the only outlet open to serious writers in the Free Zone. The column appeared weekly until the late spring of 1942, when he went to North Africa for a vacation from which he did not return. For the most part it consisted of dialogues with an imaginary journalist, the "interviews" in this volume, where they are printed in their chronological order. After the first half-dozen had been published, he wrote in his *Journal*:

*January 1, 1942*

I have gone back to work and find a semblance of happiness at my writing-desk. My thoughts are easy to formulate, so long as they aren't profound; and in my column for *Le Figaro* I have been merely stirring the surface of ideas. I have formed no judgment about events and sometimes doubt that I can play a part or find a reason for being in the new universe that is vaguely taking shape. I am certain, however, that it will have no connection with this tomfoolishness (*singerie*) of a "national revolution," which I cannot take seriously. The true heartbeats of France are hidden, and as yet they cannot afford to make themselves known. What we see, at the moment, is only a temporary show, all fraud and bluster. The ground is still too shaky for anything to be built on it. Everything depends on . . .

". . . on victory for the Allies," I suppose he meant to say; but it was dangerous to write frankly, even in one's private papers. More than a year later, in Tunis, his unpublished journals would be seized by the Ger-

mans, with the result that Gide would have to go into
hiding until the city was liberated. Meanwhile, in what
he wrote for publication in France, he was doing much
more than merely raking the topsoil of ideas. French
culture at the time was directly threatened with destruc-
tion, and not only by the invaders; it also had enemies
at home. In a modest fashion, Gide was doing his best
to preserve its living continuity.

His *Imaginary Interviews* deal with subjects like the
supposed responsibility of writers for the French defeat,
the amazing revival of poetry in an otherwise desolate
age, the rules that might govern the novel (if it had any
rules), the cast-iron traditions of French verse, and the
decay of the subjunctive mood. Reading them, one is
impressed more than ever by Gide's utter absorption in
his craft. One feels that the whole of French and European culture, past and contemporary, is simultaneously
present in his mind; that if the books were destroyed
(and many of them were unprocurable in the Free Zone),
he could supply their substance from memory. When
he makes a statement, he immediately thinks of a verse
from Racine or Baudelaire, a line from Renan or Montesquieu, to illustrate what he says; all these authors
are as much his associates as if they were sitting at the
same table helping him to judge the books of today,
which in turn belong to the same living body of art.
When he prays, late at night, it is to the great writers
still to appear. "Future values of France," he says,
"your hour will come. . . . I shall no longer be able to
hear you, and yet it is for you I am waiting."

Still, his almost religious absorption in literature does

not imply a lack of concern for other issues. Many of his remarks have political implications that must have been clear to everybody except the Germans. Mr. Varian Fry, who spent many months in the Free Zone, pointed out to me that the restrictions on free speech had produced a curious effect there: certain words in common use had become highly charged with meaning. Thus, when Gide speaks of "resistance" in quite a different connection—in several connections, as a matter of fact, for he reveals a sudden fondness for the word and always gives it a favorable connotation—his French readers can scarcely help thinking of resistance against the invaders. The word *épuration*, which means "purifying" or "purging," has also acquired a special meaning. "We hear talk of *épuration*," Gide says at one point; then he hastens to add: "Naturally we are speaking only of literature," as if to make it perfectly clear that he is thinking of other matters also. At another point the interviewer exclaims: "Long live our National Revolution, which preserves us from such a fate! It permits us to wish and hope for a general pacification." He pauses for Gide's assent, but he receives no answer. "There was a moment of silence," the author says, making his only public statement on the National Revolution.

His best thrusts at Vichy and the collaborationists take the form of literary allusions that the censors had no time to track down. Thus, when he hears that Chardonne has been praising Renan's letter to Strauss, written during the Franco-Prussian War, Gide says in a casual way that Renan wrote two letters to Strauss, both printed in a volume that he mentions by name. If

his readers referred to the volume—and we can be sure
that many of them did—they found that whereas the
first letter to Strauss was friendly in tone, the second
was a splendid philippic against the Germans. Writing
about Goethe, in one of the finest essays of our time,
Gide gives a just estimate of his achievements; but also
he condemns him for his servility to Napoleon, in words
that would be applied to any Frenchman who served
Hitler. Elsewhere his habit of making quotations from
Victor Hugo has an unmistakable meaning. Hugo, the
poet who most clearly expressed the ideals of the French
Revolution, was being abused by the critics who supported Vichy, and his works were disappearing from the
schools and even the bookshops. Gide, who had formerly
attacked Hugo, now seems to be saying: "Read him
while there is still time; read his great poems of hatred
for Napoleon the Little, and remember that every word
of them applies to our present situation." Often he seems
to be writing messages in code addressed to French pa-
triots. He has found a method of preserving his intellectual freedom and of expressing or at least implying
his thoughts in spite of the censors.

And even without these political applications his
*Imaginary Interviews* would teach a lesson that was
overlooked in the arguments over art and politics (or art
and life) that occupied much of our attention between
two wars. We were told in those days that art and politics had no connection at all; or again that they had a
most intimate connection. We were told in the 1920's
that art could not flourish unless it was pursued as a
single and separate goal; we were told in the 1930's that

it had to be subordinated to the interests of society at large (or the revolution or the masses). What nobody foresaw was that, in certain circumstances, a whole-hearted devotion to the literary art might become a political action; that it might serve, for example, as a declaration of independence from Vichy and all the tomfoolishness of a "national revolution." Simply by talking about literature, in his own subtle fashion, Gide had affirmed his belief in the older French values, including the other and genuine revolution that Vichy was trying to abolish.

The interviews were extremely difficult to translate, more so than Gide's formal prose (as in the essay on Chardonne). After all, the "high style" of the two languages is not dissimilar; but the interviews are written in a special idiom, a mixture of the literary and the colloquial, including a few slang phrases that haven't found their way into the dictionaries, and yet with every word in its proper place. Gide says, at one point in his *Journal:* "It is perfectly and obviously true that, in a fine line of verse, one cannot change or displace a word; but the same is true of fine prose. My sentences (oh, not those you find here or in many other passages of this journal) have to meet requirements that are as strict, even though they are frequently hidden, and as domineering as are those of the most rigorous prosody." Again he says, in a letter to Lady Rothermere, who wanted to translate his *Prétextes:* "The principal difficulty is that my style continually suggests rather than affirms and proceeds by insinuations—something a little repugnant to the English language, which is more direct than French. I have always felt that the ideas, in my writing, were less important than the movement of ideas"; and he adds in English: "*the gait.*" Instead of translating the *Interviews* word for word, I have therefore tried—not always with success—to achieve the same sort of movement and rightness in English.

With the exception of three added passages, to which attention is called in footnotes, the translation is based on the French text of *Interviews Imaginaires*, published in New York by Jacques Schiffrin and Company, and approved by Gide before publication. I want to thank Mr. Schiffrin and Mr. André Masson for their advice at several difficult points, without holding them responsible for the result.

Malcolm Cowley

# IMAGINARY INTERVIEW · 1

I DON'T like interviewers. They are good enough for those of other professions who may be fertile in ideas but who aren't faced with the daily task of expressing them. Men of letters can communicate directly with the public; we hardly need the help of a dragoman or interpreter who, more often than not, presents a sad travesty of our thoughts, even if he has the best intentions in the world. And yet this particular interviewer, I hardly know why, had found favor in my eyes. I had already entertained him twice. That was before the First World War, but it had created a precedent of which he took advantage on this third visit, knowing as he did that every concession is a promise for the future. I scarcely recognized him, and when he began to say that I was always the same, and really hadn't changed at all, I answered that I was tempted to take this polite falsehood for a criticism.

"What sort of reproach do you think it implies?" he asked.

"The sort that is usually phrased: 'The war hasn't taught him a single lesson.'"

"But didn't you write long ago," he said, "that the

*(3)*

shock of events merely strengthens our own predisposi-
tions?"

"I still believe it. Sometimes the shock of events also
opens our eyes to faults and vices, but they are usually
those of our neighbors."

"So long as they lead us to offer remedies . . ." he
said, letting his voice trail off. "At any rate, we try to
find remedies; and I should take for granted that you
approve of the effort."

"Yes, of course," I said.

"And doubtless you would also agree that one step
in our redemption as a nation is to offer a common ideal
to youth? That was something it lacked."

I was willing to admit that French youth, in the years
between two wars, had rushed off in all directions.

"But," he said with a half-apologetic smile, while addressing me for the first time as "dear master"—"but
didn't you add not a little to that confusion by encouraging each of us to follow his own bent?" Then, after
waiting vainly for my answer, he continued: "Wouldn't
you at least be willing to admit that our literature, generally speaking, had its own share of responsibility for
the defeat?"

Instead of giving him a direct reply, I said: "Let me
repeat a fable that is told by the natives of the Congo.
Perhaps you aren't familiar with the story.

"A great number of people, hoping to cross a broad
river, had crowded into the ferryman's boat. Overloaded,
the boat stuck fast in the mud. The question was which
of the passengers would have to get out. The ferryman
began by putting ashore a fat merchant, then a shyster

lawyer, a dishonest moneylender and the madam of a
bawdy house. The ferry didn't budge. Next to be sent
ashore were the proprietor of a gambling den, a slave-
dealer, and even a few respectable people. Still the boat
couldn't be moved, but it was getting lighter all the
time, and at last it floated when a missionary, thin as a
shadow, stepped to the bank. 'There he is,' shouted the
natives. 'There stands the very spirit of weight. May he
be accursed!' "

The interviewer asked: "Did the others climb back
into the ferry?"

"The fable doesn't say."

"Then the whole story is ridiculous," he said. "What
good is a ferryboat if nobody can ride in it?"

"The fact remains that our own ship has to be re-
floated."

"Yes, I see what you mean. There are people who say
that such and such passengers, mentioned by name, have
prevented us from crossing the river."

"And to keep the vessel afloat, they want to get rid
of them."

"Only the pure are to be left on board," he said.

"People are beginning to talk about purifying and
purging. Naturally I am speaking only of literature. It
is being accused of many crimes, including that of having
enervated, discouraged, and devitalized the nation."

"Let us admit," he said, "that many of our pre-war
writers, even the best among them, were often lacking
in—shall I say?—civic virtues."

"Weren't they reflecting the state of the country?
Moreover, they are not the only writers under attack.

We sometimes hear insults hurled at a whole period, a whole century: it was 'the stupid nineteenth century,' if we follow Léon Daudet; it was the eighteenth that deserves a pummeling, if we put our trust in Abel Bonnard. Catholic writers indict Renan, Diderot, even Montaigne; free-thinkers put the blame on Bossuet. Once more we hear the familiar chorus:

> It is the fault of Voltaire;
> It is the fault of Rousseau.

And the fault of Michelet and Hugo, adds Paul Claudel, who spits them out of his mouth."

"Lamartine," the interviewer broke in, "fell into a rage at La Fontaine, on finding that his *Fables* taught the most pernicious lessons."

"Please don't interrupt. A recent anthology of French poetry exalts our sixteenth century, but disparages the soaring flight of our Romantics, saving from all their work only a few isolated verses, a few wing-beats. That is mere derision, not judgment; and we could smile at such vain devastations, if it weren't that the books under attack are on the way to being effectively suppressed from our bookshops."

"Do you think it is really possible that . . . "

"I think anything is possible. Nothing in the world seems more childish than the cry I heard uttered so often by those who were fleeing in disorder before the invasion: 'Such a thing was never heard of.' "

"Things 'never heard of' must please you," he said, "from certain points of view."

"Yes, from certain points of view, as you observe.

And if the spectacle weren't so cruel, sometimes it would seem enthralling. But we are overwhelmed by all these novel events, these monstrous cataclysms that are 'without precedent in history.' The mind finds it hard to get used to them. The heart even more."

I was silent for some moments. The interviewer was one of the people who don't understand silences. He began again:

"A passage from Montesquieu, in the volume that Grasset has just published, might help to reassure us. I copied it out." At this he took a little notebook from his pocket. "Listen:

" 'One of the things,' " he began reading, " 'that should be noted in France is the extreme facility with which the country has always recovered from its losses, its plagues, its depopulations, and the resourcefulness with which it has always borne or even surmounted the internal vices of its different governments.' "

"Read what follows," I said. "If I remember rightly, he mentions the diversity of our country."

"Yes, for the next sentence reads: 'Perhaps this is to be explained by the very diversity of France, because of which no evil has ever been able to strike such deep roots that it could destroy entirely the fruit of her natural advantages.' "

"The passage," I said, "was not so completely unknown that I hadn't read it before. But Grasset did well to reprint it along with the others. The words are those of a sage. Nevertheless it is this diversity that is being attacked today. People would like to see it abolished."

I had risen from my chair. The interviewer said:

"Before leaving, might I ask if you are working?"

"Yes, I went back to work some weeks ago."

"Do you care to say on what?"

"First of all, on an introduction to Goethe's dramatic works, which are soon to be published by the Pléiade; in French, I am sorry to say, but the translation is a very good one. And I don't wish to treat Goethe as a mirror of myself or to search through his work for confirmation of my own ideas, including those on individualism; for perhaps those ideas came from Goethe in the first place, or at least he encouraged them. Whatever the case may be, Goethe remains for us the supreme example of a serviceable individualism. Mind you, I did not say servile, but serviceable, ready to serve. He had a deep sense of duty; yes, of duty toward himself. His apparent and evident egoism brings him back to duty and submits to duty. Those who reproach him for mere selfishness have, I think, failed to understand the austere obligations that a healthy individualism sometimes implies."

"Haven't you said all that before?"

"You make me think of a remark made by a friend of mine, also in his seventies. He had just been reproached with saying the same things over and over. 'At my age,' he replied, 'one must be willing to repeat oneself, if only to keep from talking nonsense.' "

"Is your friend by any chance a first cousin to those imaginary hangers-on whom Sainte-Beuve used to quote when he wanted to pay himself compliments?"

"You're a sly dog," I said.

"Shall I see you again?"

"It's not unlikely. Wait till I send for you."

# IMAGINARY INTERVIEW · 2

I HADN'T sent for him. Nevertheless he came back, holding in one hand the issue of *Le Figaro* in which his interview had just appeared.

"Our readers aren't satisfied," he said. "It's my own fault; I should have asked more questions. Your ideas, just as you told me, can be found in your books. The task of an interviewer is to invade your intimacy and persuade you to talk about things that you otherwise wouldn't bother to mention. It is to learn how you are and what you are doing; how you are dressed; how you manage to get enough to eat and whether you are cheerful about wartime restrictions. These are the sort of things the public expects me to write and expects me to make you say."

I hadn't the heart to refuse such a worthy man.

"If that is all you want," I said, "I shall do my best to answer you. First of all, you can set your readers' minds at rest. Tell them that it is easy enough to find people more lacking in the necessities of life than I am at present. It is true that I wear old clothes because I can't find new ones; but I take for granted that you are in the same situation. The jacket you see on my back has been relined three times and is patched at the elbows; that is what most people have had to do. As for food, there are certainly very few meals after which I shouldn't be glad to eat a beefsteak with fried potatoes; but I was pleased to learn that other French departments are somewhat better supplied than ours. On the other hand, I also know that many regions are more impoverished, and that even in the most favored districts many people are shorter than I. Fortunately it is good for my health not to eat too much meat, and I never felt better. I don't miss coffee, because I wasn't used to drinking it. The shortage from which I suffer most is, I confess, that of tobacco; for I had formed the lazy habit of smoking while I worked, which is equivalent to saying that I couldn't work without smoking. I began by thinking: What a good chance to break the habit! But I hadn't reckoned with the kindness of certain friends who, not being smokers themselves, indulged me in my vice. I am stubborn and persevering when it is a question of action, but yield easily to temptations."

*HE.*—There is a new phrase today for yielding to temptations: people call it "not saying no to life."

*I.*—Yes, I know, but I am not deceived by the sophistry. To resist is a form of action. It isn't always by saying yes that we affirm our natures. Well, are you satisfied?

*HE.*—Thank you, all this will interest the public.

*I.*—And now we can talk about serious matters.

*HE.*—Oh, there was something else I wanted to say: one remark of yours hurt me. It was when you observed that I didn't understand your silence, just after you had used the word "heart." You were mistaken. The truth is that I was surprised by the distinction you seemed to make or admit between the "heart" and the "mind." I thought you would see no difference between them. Then I happened to remember a phrase of Baudelaire's; it occurs in his *Artificial Paradises,* in the chapter "On Wine and Hashish." Having written "the heart," Baudelaire at once corrected himself and added: "or rather the human brain." But I thought you were like Valéry and disapproved of fuzzy words.

*I.*—No, I think we couldn't do without them. "Heart," "mind" . . . it is clear enough what we mean by such words, even when they aren't easy to define. They are merely vague at the edges, which tend to overlap. Certain emotions are partly intellectual and certain ideas are emotive. It may be that without the intellect we should have no emotions at all, and hence no sentiments or passions. But even so, we feel that a surge of blood to the brain comes straight from the heart, and we cannot fail to recognize some appeals from the brain that make the heart beat faster. By all means let us keep both words or we shall be lost completely. And it is the same with other words, like "soul" and "God"; with all the big words that are imprecise, it is true—but isn't that the reason why they are useful? Certainly the phrase "my country," to mention one example, does not suggest the same landscapes to peasants in Picardy and to those in Provence; it is not understood in the same fashion by the plowman and the poet, by the poor and the rich. But still it is a rallying cry. And when we hear that our country is in danger, the next step is to rise as one man to defend it; even if what we defend may be [1] specifically, for the peasant, our cultivated fields; for the poet, our culture in general; for the manufacturer and the workman, our industrial wealth; and even, for the stockholder, his own dividends. The phrase "my country" includes all these different elements; both the mind and the heart know what it means.

I wish I could say as much for the word "love," since its careless use often leads to serious confusion. What exists in common between the scriptural love of one's neighbor that implies the gift of oneself, and the unbridled appetite, the lust for possession that often leads to crime? Aren't you troubled by hearing some of our Romantics apply the same word, "beloved," to mother, daughter, or sister indiscriminately?

*HE.*—We can depend on psychologists to draw the necessary distinctions.

*I.*—Whereupon they are accused of splitting hairs. But I have to confess that nature herself often changes the signposts to lead us astray. There are secret bypaths from one sort of love to another; there are transformations and misunderstandings. Sometimes, if rarely, carnal desire becomes disembodied, while an aspiration that began by being ethereal will end in corruption.

*HE.*—Or perhaps you mean to say: "will end in fulfillment."

*I.*—It is true that love can occupy spirit and body at

---

[1] At this point Gide, the purist, uses the subjunctive *soit* in an "if" clause, thus committing what is sometimes regarded as a grave error in French grammar. But see the following interview.—Tr.

the same time. In many cases, however, one of them profits at the expense of the other, and this may lead to painful tragedies, since either spirit or body is frustrated. . . . But I am wandering far afield.

*HE*.—I am here to listen.

*I.*—Yes, but I would rather not wander too far. Our literature is excessively preoccupied with such matters, and Jean Schlumberger was right to deplore its continual emphasis on love. The mistake he made in that same article was to put the blame on Racine. He wasn't entirely correct even when he said that love was the mainspring of almost all Racine's tragedies; or at least he should have added that they almost always picture love as being held in check by other interests. Let him remember what Titus said to Bérénice:

*Je sens bien que sans vous je ne saurais plus vivre . . .*
*Mais il ne s'agit plus de vivre, il faut régner.*

—"Without you I feel that I cannot longer live . . . And yet my duty now is not to live, but reign." And after condemning Racine, what would Schlumberger have to say about the plays of Marivaux and Musset, where love reigns supreme and has no rival? From reading many French authors, by no means the least important, we might deduce that love is man's ultimate goal, that all his achievements lead to it, end in it, and are consumed in it; that nothing but love deserves our interest and that there are no characters worth presenting in the whole world but lovers and mistresses. And if only they were exalted by love, as sometimes happens in life; if only it impelled men to heroism, women to virtue, and both to some flowering of all their qualities that could not be attained in isolation and that, without the wakening of love, they might never have glimpsed! . . . But for one *Princesse de Clèves*, there are a hundred *Manon Lescauts*.

*HE*.—Take care! You too are beginning to cry shame and call for ostracism.

*I*.—No, I admire *Manon Lescaut*, but I should like such books to serve as guard-ropes at the edge of deep water. This one is deeply felt and is written in a natural style. Therefore we are tempted to exaggerate its importance, which is great enough in any case.

*HE*.—Wouldn't you say that France alone could have produced this masterpiece?

*I*.—Masterpiece! You are going a little too far. That France alone could have given birth to it I am willing to grant, but with a shade of regret. In any case, still speaking of *Manon*, I doubt that any other country could have furnished it with such a deplorable abundance of offspring. Don't misunderstand me. It is not the depiction of loose morals or evil surroundings that I object to in a novel; it is the flabbiness, the slackness. Take the example of Sartre, who is using his extraordinary talent to present us with pictures of depravity; he is never flabby. For that he deserves great credit. But with what relief I turn back to *Moby Dick* or *Robinson Crusoe*. Unfortunately there has been no equivalent in French literature for virile works like these . . . until now, at any rate.

*HE*.—You might also have mentioned Stevenson's

*Treasure Island* and several novels by Joseph Conrad. But you say: "until now." Do you mean to suggest that . . . ?

*I.*—Yes, I intended to mention the works of Giono, Malraux, Saint-Exupéry and Montherlant, among others. They fill me with hope that we are leaving the rut in which so many of our writers seemed to enjoy being mired; that we are about to stand erect after rising from what Baudelaire called those "divans deep as tombs." Dignity, heroism, and nobility of heart find their echoes, I believe, among the new generation.

*HE.*—Excuse me, but didn't you once write that fine sentiments make bad literature?

*I.*—I have often been reproached for that phrase by people who didn't understand what it meant and who, for the most part, quoted it incorrectly, besides forgetting that I had written *Strait Is the Gate,* which may have pointed too stern a moral for their tastes. "He alleges," so they alleged of me, "that evil always triumphs in works of art. But we know better, having read good novels like *The Coming Harvest* and *The Roquevillards.*" [2]

That good intentions can't take the place of genius was about all I wanted to say; the hell of literature (for which read "inferior literature") is paved with them. These stupidly edifying books are not only mediocre in themselves, but they also discredit everything they try

[2] *Le Blé qui lève,* by René Bazin (1907) and *Les Roquevillard,* by Henry Bordeaux (1906). Both novels were extremely popular in right-thinking families.—Tr.

to extol; and a virtuous drama like *The Daughter of Roland* leads by way of protest to *The Parisienne* and *Woman in Love* [3] . . . to mention only the best.

We were silent for a few moments, while I crumbled the butts of four cigarettes to roll another.

*HE.*—I noticed, though I didn't dare to interrupt you, that you said "shorter than I," when speaking of the food rations; and then, a little later, that you used the subjunctive after an "if." . . . Was that by inadvertence?

*I.*—No. But enough for today. We can speak of that another time.

---

[3] *La Parisienne,* by Henry Becque (1885) and *Amoureuse,* by Georges de Porto-Riche (1891), two plays that lived up to their titles. *La Fille de Roland* (1875) was a drama in verse by Henri de Bornier.—Tr.

# IMAGINARY INTERVIEW · 3

THAT afternoon I was in high good humor, for I had managed to buy two packages of cigarettes on the same day. Ever since we have been *short of tobacco*, it is curious how good it seems to smoke.

As soon as he came in, my interviewer was at it again. What he wanted to talk about was the expression that had surprised him during his last visit.

"It was the right word to use," I answered. "You might have learned as much by reading the column called 'Anti-Littré' [1] that appears in your own newspaper. To be frank, that is how I learned it. But I should like to argue just a little with *Le Figaro's* learned and entertaining columnist. He was dealing with two different expressions, *être à court* (literally, 'to be *at* short') [2] and *être court* ('to be short'). Now, I should say to him, let us admit that the first of these expressions, *être à court*—of

---

[1] Emile Littré (1801–81) was the great lexicographer. His *Dictionnaire* is still standard for French usage, even if *Figaro's* columnist likes to quarrel with it.—Tr.

[2] In this third interview, which involves some of the intricacies of French grammar, all words enclosed in parentheses are supplied by the translator.—Tr.

*(17)*

money, fuel, munitions, or arguments—was the one singled out by Littré as being incorrect. Let us admit that it is being generally used instead of the quite legitimate *être court,* to be short of this or that, with the result that the latter expression now runs the risk of seeming archaic or affected; and besides it tends to be confined, or such is my impression, to a somewhat different sense from what it had in the beginning. *Etre court de tabac* now means to have very little tobacco; *être à court de tabac* means to have none at all."

"With the result," my interviewer said, "that the latter expression, if I understand you correctly, cannot be used in the comparative."

"That is another reason why I said 'shorter than I.' Since the French Academy and Littré too regard the word 'short' as an adjective, shouldn't it come under the rules that govern adjectives in general?"

He said: "I should be curious to know what Anti-Littré thinks about it."

" 'But if Littré were living today,' I should say to the columnist who is quarreling with his ghost, 'don't you think he would find good reasons for granting freedom of the city to this *à court de* that shocks you? Don't you think that the other expression, the correct *court de,* doesn't exactly take its place? You will have to admit,' I should tell him, 'that you have no power to change what has become the general usage, and that a language whose rules are fixed is a language that is dead. Littré himself, by the examples he quoted from the current speech of his time, authorized the use of certain words that had lost their original meaning: for example, *mièvre* (which has come to mean "dainty" or "prim," and which nobody uses in its original sense of "roguish"), as well as idioms which at first seemed incorrect, but became sound currency after some standard author had used them. I was thinking of *depuis* (in English, "since" or "from"), which wasn't supposed to be used except in expressions of time; we said "*depuis* 1800," but I was shocked to read on Swiss postcards that they showed a view of Mont Blanc *depuis* Geneva. I have almost lost this feeling, however, *depuis* the time when Barrès was bold enough to write *depuis la fenêtre* (from the window) and *depuis* the Chamber of Deputies; and scores of writers have followed his example.

" 'Moreover,' I should say to Anti-Littré, whoever he may be, 'aren't you afraid of frightening off the foreigners who would like to learn our language, when you make it seem so difficult?'

" 'No,' the gentleman would answer—and I hope he will forgive me for putting these words in his mouth. 'Not when you consider that the faults I point out are taken from the work of eminent writers. Isn't it reassuring rather than otherwise to know that great men have nodded?'

" 'Do you think it wise,' I should then ask him, 'to make a fuss over trifles, at a time when so many glaring errors, which you are discreet enough not to mention, stand out from our almost official texts and startle us when we listen to the government radio?' "

At this the interviewer broke into my dialogue. "For my part," he said, "I should prefer to ask: 'Do you think it wise to linger over these futilities at a time when we are harassed by such grave problems and when our vital interests . . .' "

*I.*—Stop there. Why do you say futilities? Questions of language impress me as having the greatest importance. I take it for a good sign that intellectuals are concerned about them; that they continue to argue over words in the midst of the wildest confusion and the most tragic disasters; it is fortunate indeed that their debates are followed with passionate interest by thousands of Frenchmen. Were it not for curiosity, expectation, and hope, it might seem to most of us that death was the best solution for our troubles. But we should prefer when dying to leave behind us a daily speech that wasn't totally corrupted. The language, at every stage in the life of a nation, is discreetly revealing. One sign, for example, is the decay of the subjunctive, something I began to complain about during the other war. The subjunctive is the mood that indicates a certain type of connection between two statements, a dependence of one on the other, a subordination for which people have ceased to recognize the need.

*HE.*—In England the subjunctive disappeared a long time ago, leaving hardly more than traces.

*I.*—Precisely. British self-dependence.

*HE.*—Whatever the case may be, such questions are of interest only to educated people.

*I.*—There you are wrong. The working classes are sensitive to questions of language, and they know how to recognize the proper word, even in slang. Do you remember that charming scene of Marcel Achard's in which two friends fall out?—and all because one of them says to the other: "I get along with you like a sardine does with oil," while the second insists that "like a sardine with oil" would be enough.

*HE.*—Now you are joking.

*I.*—I was never more serious. Habits of speech are revealing, as I said. A nation that stands by its language stands firm. But let us get back to the subjunctive.

It is true that there was one point in our last conversation when the subjunctive after *si*—if—seemed to me, in that one connection, both possible and justified. Anti-Littré would perhaps condemn it there as elsewhere. I felt, however, that the indicative would have given a false shade of meaning to what I was trying to say. The French *si* has always been a stumbling-block to foreigners; logically it should be followed by a verb in the subjunctive or the conditional, as in many other languages. Even when a foreigner speaks quite passable French, he is likely to say, and almost certain to think he is right in saying: *Si j'aurais* or *si je devrais y aller* —"If I should have" or "if I should go there" (instead of simply "If I have" or "if I go there").

*HE.*—It is correct to say: *Je ne sais si je* devrais *y aller*—"I don't know if I really should go."

*I.*—Obviously. But that isn't the sort of thing I was talking about. It is a sentence in which one would use the conditional *devrais* even without the *si;* the implication being that you *should* go there and really don't feel up to it. The *si* isn't what determines the form of the verb. On the other hand, only a foreigner would say: *Si j'en* aurais *le courage je partirais*—"If I *should feel* up to it, I should go."

*HE.*—A foreigner is also puzzled by the use of the present tense after *si* in statements having to do with the future. Where we say: *S'il fait beau temps demain* —"If it's a nice day tomorrow"—he is tempted to say: "If it *will be* a nice day."

*I.*—We ourselves are puzzled by the Englishman's fashion of saying: "When I am old"; he uses the present tense where French requires the future. But listen to this: I found in Victor Hugo a marvelous example of the future employed after *si*. It occurs in a poem called "Claire," printed in his *Contemplations:*

> *Qui donc attendons-nous s'ils ne reviendront pas?*

—"Then whom are we waiting for, if they *will not return?*" Hugo was a poet who could safely take liberties with the language, for he never broke a rule except to produce an astonishing effect.

But let us get back to the subjunctive. It seems to be disappearing, and already there are many French writers—I am not thinking merely of worthless scribblers—who seem to have lost their instinct for using it. Chiefly this fact becomes evident when the subjunctive is distinguished from the indicative only by the accent over a vowel. Between the indicative *fait* and the subjunctive *fasse*—"makes" and "make"—there is an audible difference; but, in the past imperfect of the same verb, the ear makes no distinction between *fît and fît*. Many people who say correctly: *Le temps qu'il* fait, and *Je sortirai quelque temps qu'il* fasse—"The sort of weather it *is*," and "I shall leave the house no matter what the weather *may be*"—also say correctly, when speaking of yesterday's weather: *Le temps qu'il* fit *hier,* and *Quelque temps qu'il* fît; but they write the last word without the circumflex that is here the distinguishing mark of the subjunctive, because the sound of the vowel does not warn them that the verb is in a different mood. They employ the subjunctive unwittingly, confusing it with the indicative; and the result is that I am expecting very soon to hear: *Je sortirai quelque temps qu'il* fait (instead of *fasse*).

Would you like me to show you some examples to illustrate what I have just been saying? I found them in Proust, an extraordinary subtle writer, but one in whose work such errors abound.

*HE.*—It is always comforting to hear about other people's mistakes.

*I.*—Let me have the third volume of *Sodome et Gomorrhe* II; it's there on the shelf and I have marked the pages. Here we are on page 13: *"M. de Charlus ne s'inquiétait pas que Madame Verdurin* fut *debout"* (instead of *fût*). On page 51, *"J'avais peur qu'elle ne* prit *froid"* (instead of *prît*). Time after time he omits the circumflex that marks the subjunctive mood. On page 62, ". . . *n'ayant même pas l'air de supposer qu'il* put *y avoir doute sur notre réponse."* On page 69, *"Et qui* eut *regardé en ce moment Morel* . . . eut *compris."* On page 83, *"J'*eus *été celui pour qui l'on se cache de tout."* On page 97, *"La compagnie désirait qu'il* revint *au plus vite à Paris."* On page 137, ". . . *afin que mon oncle ne* put *être froissé."* Not wishing to be repetitious, I pass over scores of similar examples. But I can't help noting a still more curious fact: that Proust, on the

other hand, is capable of using the circumflex precisely
where it is not required: "*Aussitôt qu'il fût là*" (instead
of *fut*), on page 156, and "*Or dès qu'il* fût *entré à pas de
loup dans le vestibule,*" on page 166. And this strange
need for employing the subjunctive where it doesn't belong is even more evident when the word has a different
form: "*Bien que je ne sache pas pourquoi on* aille *sur
ces routes-ci,*" on page 194 (where *va* instead *aille*
would be the correct form).

*HE.*—A good proofreader would have corrected all
that.

*I.*—You can rest assured that he does correct it for
scores of authors and that Proust is far from being the
only one to fall into errors of the sort. Moreover, a good
proofreader puts a question mark in the margin beside
doubtful words: as he might, or should, have done beside the word *louche,* which Proust twice employs as an
adjective, on pages 29 and 31: "*le marquis était* louche"
and "*je fus monté en ascenseur . . . par le chasseur*
louche," to indicate that both the marquis and the bell-
boy *louchaient* (that they squinted; whereas the adjective *louche* would imply that the bell-boy, at least, was
morally rather than physically cross-eyed). He should
also have put a question mark beside "*Je crois qu'Albertine eût* insupporté *maman,*" in volume I, page 17, of
*La Prisonnière* (where Proust means to say that his
mother couldn't have supported Albertine); and beside
"*un instrument nouvellement inventé dont il ne savait
pas l'usage et* dont *il n'ose pas commencer à manger,*"
on page 40 of the same volume (where *avec lequel,* rather
than *dont,* is the logical expression to use). Without

consulting the author, he should have corrected *proh-éminent* (for *proéminent*), page 48, and *la loi causable*, on page 88 (since *causable* is not a French word). He should—but why go on?

*HE.*—All in all, you seem to feel that a good proof-reader must know more French than the author himself.

*I.*—That is part of his trade.

*HE.*—And yet you regard Proust as a great writer.

*I.*—Very great and one of the most important.

*HE.*—This seems to imply that, in your judgment, a man can be a great writer without being a correct writer.

*I.*—The two don't necessarily go together; and Voltaire was a hundred times right when he said that he valued

> A genius' impropriety
> More than the chill exactness of
> A purist of the Academy.

We even find today that the faults and impropriety of genius were what he valued too little. But I should doubt that there were many great writers who did not show an admirable mastery of the language; who were not able to utilize and profit from its resources while observing its rules, even if they sometimes manhandled them.

*HE.*—Aren't there many grammatical errors in Saint-Simon as well as in Proust?

*I.*—They are due to the leaps and bounds of his pen. Yet Stendhal wrote just as fast, just as impetuously, without rereading his manuscripts, and I hardly think that one could find many such errors in his novels. . . . But wait until Anti-Littré has shaken them through his fine sieve. No more for today, if you please.

# IMAGINARY INTERVIEW · 4

I was working when the interviewer came in. "Is it still that introduction to Goethe's dramatic works?" he said.

"It might turn out to be disappointing," I told him. "I have been reading Goethe ever since I was twenty, but it is hard for me to write a proper introduction without referring to books that aren't to be found outside of Paris. André Billy was right to complain about the poverty of our French provincial bookshops. Lacking the texts, I shall have to confine myself to generalities and to what I can remember from my reading. After all, it may be better for the essayist, as it is for the novelist, not to work directly from the facts, but rather to let them be sifted through our memories, which retain only the essentials. This at any rate is what I say to keep myself from losing heart, while knowing all the time that the facts in themselves are unique and irreplaceable. But here as elsewhere, and always, we have to play with the cards in our hands.

"The lack of books," I continued, "will be a more serious drawback when I try to complete the anthology

on which I have been working these many years; for that
will require the poems themselves."

*HE.*—Other anthologies have recently been published,
and their favorable reception by the public confirms the
prediction you made when answering a questionnaire.
You said, if I remember correctly, that we might expect
a rebirth of lyric poetry. Collections of verse are spring-
ing up on all sides, and the public, for the first time, has
seized on them greedily.

*I.*—It would seem that poetry has become a refuge.

*HE.*—Let us hope that the new anthologies edited
by Thierry-Maulnier, by Marcel Arland, and by Jean
Prévost haven't caused you to abandon your own project?

*I.*—Mine won't resemble them in the least; it will be
the answer to very different needs. I am sure that all
three books you mentioned are extremely well edited,
although I have seen only the first two; but I have to
confess that both of them left me unsatisfied. Like most
of the earlier anthologies, they have apparently taken
it upon themselves to justify the reputation we have
gained in foreign countries, that of allowing our Parnassus to be invaded by orators; where you hoped for
music, instead you find logic and eloquence. Thierry-
Maulnier's anthology displays an excessively personal
judgment, which helps to explain the great interest
aroused by his book; it is a profession of faith. In his
introduction he reveals a lamentable zeal and the blind
ferocity of a partisan; he expresses himself by what he
condemns. While overpraising the poets he admires, he
is content to give paltry and fallacious reasons for dis-

missing the others. Very often he makes me feel that, in
spite of everything he says, the reasons are essentially
political (I am using the word in its broadest sense),
just as in other cases they are essentially religious. If
we hope to enjoy poetry, we must for a time abandon
all such considerations; the reader should approach it
with an open mind. That is one reason why, in these days,
it can have such a tonic effect.

*HE.*—Speaking of your own anthology, might I ask
what principles will govern your choice of poems?

*I.*—They will be explained in a preface. But, properly
speaking, they can't be called principles at all. Let us
say that I shall try not to lay too much emphasis on my
personal taste and that I shan't yield to such momentary
and unwise reactions as the one that caused Thierry-
Maulnier to overlook Chénier and Moréas and Verlaine,
while perching Maynard "at a lyric height that Lamartine and Hugo never dreamed of reaching" and omitting
all but a few lines of Hugo in order to find more space
for Gérard de Nerval. Most assuredly he was right to
restore Nerval and Maurice Scève [1] to their proper
places, considering that both men have suffered from a
prolonged and unjustified neglect. But, to judge by the
tendencies of certain critics, it is Hugo himself, that

---

[1] Maynard and Scève are typical in their different fashions of the
poets who have been exalted by the French traditionalists. Maurice
Scève (1510?–1564?) was a learned alderman of Lyon and the leader
of a flourishing school of poets there. At his best he suggests John
Donne, but he wrote in an alembicated style and until recently his
work was read only by scholars. François Maynard (1582–1646) was
one of the "Grammarians" who followed Malherbe. This master said
of him that, among all his disciples, Maynard was the one who wrote
the best verse, but that there was little vigor in his work.—Tr.

master of lyricism, the greatest in our pantheon, who is
becoming a neglected poet. Do they think that the few
poems by Hugo still grudgingly quoted in the school-
books or in recent anthologies are enough even to suggest the resources of his inexhaustible genius? "It was
purely a verbal genius," so we are told. What a prepos-
terous notion! And how silly to speak of Hugo's "stu-
pidity"! He proved his intelligence by never allowing
his verse to be overburdened with or crippled by ideas.
Everything is subordinated to the plenitude of his verse;
even his emotion, which I cannot say is always very sincere; it is as if he had seized upon and applied to himself Diderot's paradox about the actor: that his task is
not to be moved by emotion, but to move others. Or perhaps we could say that the emotion comes first, inspiring
the verse; then a moment later the verse itself is exalting
and inflating the emotion. But what verse! And except
for creating verse, why else does he live and think and
feel? One might say that the rhymes, those wild birds
(and there were some rhymes he disdained to use because they had been too long domesticated), gathered
from the four corners of the horizon to seize the crumbs
of intellectual nourishment that he held out to them;
in the same way we sometimes see a flock of sparrows or
pigeons fluttering round a bird-tamer in our public gardens. I concede that there are some of his enormous poems
from which whole sections crumble, being built of lath
and plaster; but even so one comes across jewels gleam-
ing among the ruins. It is a pleasure to look for them,
and I have almost never done so without finding some
reward. Listen: in one of the worst, the most painful

sections of the bewildering and tedious *Bouche d'ombre*, there suddenly gleams this extraordinary line:

*Il descend, réveillé, l'autre côté du rêve*

—"He wakens and descends the other slope of dream"; it is a verse so pregnant with such a brilliant image, so eloquent of intermingled thought and emotion, that you would seek vainly for its equal elsewhere than in Hugo. I agree that when the colossus wants to "play the man" (in the same sense that Pascal said "play the angel" or "play the beast") and tries to present himself simply as a lover, a father, or a grandfather, he is often at his worst. It is your privilege, moreover, to prefer the human to the gigantesque. But instead of demanding qualities from people that we could easily find elsewhere, should we not take them for what they are: the titans for titans, the dwarfs for dwarfs, and the pedants who attack Hugo for fools? The other day you and I were talking about the bad French sometimes written by great authors. You will never find Hugo writing incorrectly or falling into grammatical errors, faulty syntax, weakness of vocabulary, or simple awkwardness. He is never halted or hindered by the difficulties of French prosody or of the language in general; he hurdles each obstacle and transforms each grammatical rule into a springboard. . . . Why did you let me talk so long?

*HE.*—I was listening. But if you have finished your tribute to Hugo, I am curious to know why you once said, when asked who was the greatest French poet: "Hugo, alas!"

*I.*—I would say it again. However great my admiration for Hugo, I am ill at ease with his bombast, feeling as I do that it is always artificial, that it rhymes with nothing; or rather that it does nothing else but rhyme. His thoughts seem to drift at the mercy of his verse, as if on a mountain torrent; and they make me wish for more rigor and authenticity. You understand, of course, that I am speaking of Hugo only as a lyric poet, being little concerned with his novels and even less with his dramas, now that we have ceased to be imposed upon by their flagrant artifice. Moreover, if we reserve a place apart for his *Things Seen* (and for everything else of his that might have been published under the same title), in which he shows himself to be a marvelous reporter, we find elsewhere that often, all too often,

> *Ses yeux plongent plus loin que le monde réel*

—that his eyes see beyond the real world. But let him only deal with that world and he is able, when he so desires, to see and depict it admirably. I might add that he is a master of invective.

*HE.*—If Hugo came back to earth, he would doubtless be astonished to learn that his vast output is being balanced against Baudelaire's one book of verse, and that many of our best critics, abroad as in France, have chosen to praise the latter.

*I.*—I too should vote for Baudelaire; but only after having saluted Hugo the enormous with an enormous bow.

My interviewer took these last words for a hint and rose to go.

*I.*—Before you leave, I wanted to ask one question: Have you seen the poems of Lil Boels?

*HE.*—Isn't she the young woman who has been reciting her own ballads in a little music hall near the Place d'Italie? They say that everybody in Paris has been crowding in to hear them. The only thing of hers I have read is the poem that is supposed to serve as a preface to her collection, I mean the one that was printed a few days ago in *Le Figaro*.

*I.*—Well, what did you think of it?

The interviewer assumed a knowing look that revealed his total ignorance of the subject.

*HE.*—There were some things in it that I thought weren't bad at all.

*I.*—That weren't bad! I want you to know that the poem is excellent. If only her book, *Fosse Commune*,[2] which I hear will be published soon, has many lines as remarkable as these, for example:

> *M'man souffrait que j'soye maladive*
> *que j'parlais pas et jouais jamais,*
> *elle d'vinait qu' ça m'rendait pensive*
> *et m'donnait des chagrins secrets.*

> *J'cherchais, dans les fêt's de famille,*
> *la tristess' du jour qui suivrait.*

---

[2] *Potter's Field* might be its English title. Note that Mlle Boels, in her eight-syllable lines, violates the rules of French verse by counting only the syllables that would be pronounced in ordinary conversation; instead of *je soye* and *devinait,* she writes *j'soye* and *d'vinait.* Popular ballads are often written in this fashion. For the classical laws of French prosody, see the Appendix.

Incidentally, the passage about Lil Boels, though printed in *Le Figaro,* does not appear in the French text of *Interviews Imaginaires.*—Tr.

> *j'cherchais l'caillou dans les lentilles,*
> *et les araignées dans l'rosier.*
>
> *J'ai fait ça sur un' grande échelle*
> *tout' ma vie et c'est d'venu d'la*
>     *déformation professionnelle.*
> *C'est trop tard, j' m'en corrig'rai pas* . . .

Mother was worried for, oh, I was
A sickly brat and I played alone
And scarcely talked and it made her feel
That I surely had sorrows all my own.

On Sunday picnics I sat by myself
Thinking of toothaches and Monday woes;
I looked for the pebbles among the peas,
I looked for a spider inside the rose.

Always I followed these recipes
In sunshine and storm, till they became
    my occupational disease.
It's too late now, I won't ever reform.

*HE.*—I might as well say frankly that I detest the trivial style in verse.

*I.*—You could hardly detest it more than I do. If these stanzas were just a little less good, I should find them intolerable. But I can say that (except for those of Aragon, in their very different fashion) I have read no poems for a long time that seemed to me better, or even as good, or that affected me more. I was not surprised to hear that Léon-Paul Fargue likes them; he is the best of judges, and you can take his word for their quality, if you won't take mine. Poems in the trivial style, as you call it, are usually compounded of pure affectation, but this one rings true.

*HE.*—And her systematic elision of the mute "e's"—it doesn't give you gooseflesh?

*I.*—Such elision is natural; it follows the example of our daily speech. Poets are using an artifice, on the other hand, when they assign the same metrical value to syllables that would be silent in conversation and to those that are fully pronounced.

*HE.*—The artifice is one that all our best poets have employed for their most exquisite effects.

*I.*—But still it amazes foreigners, for it remains peculiar to the French language, and they have a hard time training their ears to enjoy it. What seems to me more serious is that it has been tending more and more to separate the people at large from our classical poetry, based as it is on the traditional laws of verse. Our best poets are no longer understood, except by a very small number of people.

*HE.*—And this you regard as a great pity. But might I be permitted to ask: a pity for the people or for the poets? Do you think that the latter should now be seeking a wider audience?

*I.*—At our next meeting, I shall try to answer your question.

# IMAGINARY INTERVIEW · 5

"Do you know how many there are?" he asked me without waiting to catch his breath.

*I.*—How many what?

*HE.*—French poets writing today, if you please. According to a recent article in the *Cahiers de la Jeune France*, André Billy was astonished to find that there were no less than a hundred. But Henri de Lescoët offered to show Billy a more inclusive list, one that cites the names of "exactly two hundred poet-poets, known and living."

*I.*—Known?

*HE.*—Known to him, in any case.

*I.*—Merciful heavens! Did you say two hundred? We didn't ask for so many.

*HE.*—If you don't call that a renaissance . . .

*I.*—Setting aside a score or more of those we could name, who belong to the declining generation and are ready to surrender their places, in addition to perhaps a dozen of the newer poets who have been able to gain our attention, I should guess that the greater part of the poet-poets in this admirable list are still under thirty.

*HE.*—I should hope so. They are the "future vigor" of which Rimbaud spoke.

*I.*—And that leads me on to another remark. If somebody had made a similar list in the year 1900, it would not only have been much shorter, but it would have omitted the names of Claudel and Péguy, who hadn't yet given us any poem-poems, not to mention that of Paul Valéry, who, after some youthful verses, had chosen to subside into a prolonged silence. And yet in 1900 all three of these poets had reached or passed their thirtieth year.

*HE.*—What are you driving at?

*I.*—Why, simply at this: that the most important poet living today, the poet who will be discussed tomorrow and honored by younger poets as a worthy link in a memorable chain—that perhaps he is not even mentioned in the list, being still hidden in the shadows where fate holds him in reserve. It is a great and rare virtue to be patient, to wait and ripen, to correct oneself, to begin over again and, as the apostle said, to strive toward perfection. But the desire for perfection is being lost, and more's the pity. It was a real French quality.

At this my interviewer made a rather ingenious remark and one, I confess, that surprised me as coming from him.

*HE.*—These are times when the desire for the perfect seems to have taken refuge in the world of mechanical instruments, where perfection can be measured by utility and the rate of production. In the realm of art, on the other hand, there are no fixed standards.

*I.*—Yes, in painting and poetry, in everything personal, the artist and the public are satisfied today with hasty affirmations and sometimes with mere daubs. At times this tendency seems to reveal a certain love for the formless. There is no question today of masterpieces; the word itself sounds a little absurd. There is no question of permanence; all bets are being placed on the moment.

*HE.*—Mightn't it be that our future seems too uncertain?

*I.*—The masters chosen by young writers today are those whose genius poured over its banks like a flooded river. It is the absence of dikes that fascinates their disciples; hence a certain contempt for restraint, for effort. They let themselves go and call it genius. Talent has to be acquired, but nobody bothers to acquire it. I remember having written a long time ago that it takes a lot of talent to make a little genius bearable.

*HE.*—I'm not quite sure of whom you are speaking.

*I.*—Neither am I.

As I had nothing more to say at the moment, the interviewer resumed the discussion.

*HE.*—This striving for perfection, which you said was such a French quality, has often been reckoned against us by less cultivated nations, by more impulsive and simple-minded peoples. They regard it as evidence of arrested growth and a yearning for the past; for they say that nothing can be perfected unless it has ceased to grow and that whatever is developing cannot be fixed or polished.

*I.*—Let us rather say that whatever is fixed in its place to be perfected thereby ceases to develop. Yes, I can repeat all those maxims and I have learned to distinguish, even in the twanging of rude and ill-tuned lyres, an effort toward new harmonies not yet reduced to a system. There is no renaissance that doesn't begin by bursting its husk, like a ripening seed. Yesterday's perfection must be shattered for tomorrow's harvest. . . . After a brief search, I could perhaps find less hackneyed metaphors. I might play on the two senses of the word "finished."

*HE.*—You like to play on words.

*I.*—Indeed yes, for that is how they reveal their wealth of meaning. But you interrupted me when I still wanted to point out that— Oh, yes, it was about a line from André Chénier:

*Sur des pensers nouveaux faisons des vers antiques*

—"With newborn thoughts let us make ancient verse"; I wanted to say that, in spite of this precept, newborn thoughts don't enter the temple of Art in borrowed raiment. The point of perfection is reached only when the novelty of the form corresponds exactly to the inner novelty. Now, we are all too much inclined in such cases to remain insensible to both novelties; whereas we are disposed to regard as perfect a form that we *recognize*, even when this "old bottle" is not the proper receptacle for the "new wine" it contains. We don't hesitate to dismiss as formless an entirely new style, a quite unprecedented form (whether it is assumed by a poem, a sonata or a picture), even when the form is rendered inevitable by the novelty of its content, from which it cannot be separated and with which it is indissolubly mingled. For we are blundering into an old and absurd quarrel when we try to consider "form" apart from "matter"; the truth is

that they are, or should be, the same thing. Either the
poetic renaissance will create new forms or it will not
exist. Every true artist creates his proper form, just as
a mollusc secretes its own armor. May Apollo guard our
Parnassus from the hermit crabs of art that live in borrowed shells!

At this the interviewer timidly reminded me that nevertheless the sonnet—to mention one form among others—
had not been invented by Shakespeare any more than by
Ronsard, Michelangelo, or Petrarch; and that for a long
time afterwards a multitude of poets, including the
greatest and the best, in their several countries, had been
able to pour their genius into this conventional mold.

His remark was so pertinent that my thoughts, desert-
ing the position they had taken, at once began to move in
this new direction. It suddenly seemed clear to me that,
if there were no names in the history of art except those
belonging to the creators of new forms, there would be
no more culture; the very word implied a continuity, and
therefore it called for disciples, imitators, and followers
to make a living chain: in other words, a tradition. I felt
nonplussed and, fearing to reveal my confusion, I alleged
a sudden fatigue. As for the question he had asked during
the previous interview, on the subject of popular poetry,
I needed more time to think it over. I begged him to come
back another day.

After he was gone, I sat there deep in thought. Yes,
going back to our discussion and to what I had said
about the need for greater ripeness, I meditated for a
long time on the younger writers who are now holding
their peace and allowing their thoughts and their quali-

ties of heart to be fortified little by little in solitude and silence. And I felt a prayer rising from my heart to my lips, an uncertain and trembling prayer: "Have patience for yet a little while. Future values of France, your hour will come"—an ardent prayer for those who will speak out when perhaps I shall not be there to listen. I shall no longer be able to hear you, and still it is for you I am waiting.

# IMAGINARY INTERVIEW · 6

As soon as he came in, he began to cross-examine me about popular poetry, besides reproaching me for putting off the subject from one week to the next—so that his readers, he said, were getting impatient; for it was now a burning question. You would gather from his remarks that poets in general were waiting for my verdict before addressing themselves to the masses or retiring into private worlds. I was to tell him on the spot whether I thought that poetry was going to become popular and whether I approved of this development; whether poetry should draw closer to the masses or the masses closer to poetry, and which of the two would profit more—for after all, he said, wasn't this the tendency revealed by the undoubted poetic renaissance it was now our consoling privilege to witness? . . . His remarks were so confused that at first I hardly knew what to answer. It almost seemed that the interviewer himself was suffering from a sort of lyric frenzy.

"It must be recognized," I ventured after he had grown a little calmer, "that the relations between our public and our poets have always been somewhat strained."

"But today," he answered, "all that seems likely to change, don't you think? Cruel defeats have unified our people. This communion, first in sorrow and then in hope, makes us all feel the presence of a sort of joint soul."

*I.*—So I have heard. But I believe, if I may be permitted to speak frankly, that the unification of minds you so admire is much more apparent than real; much more a hope than a fulfillment. Although stricken by a common misfortune, the French remain as divided as ever.

*HE.*—If that is true, don't you find it distressing?

*I.*—No. We have often been told that the value of France consisted in her diversity. Must I remind you of the passage from Montesquieu that you insisted on reading to me not so long ago?

*HE.*—But wouldn't you agree that the task of a great poet, just at this time, would be to raise the minds and hearts of all Frenchmen to the same pitch of enthusiasm?

*I.*—Now I see what's coming: you are going to say that our age deserves a new Béranger.

*HE.*—Oh, we have the right to expect something better than that.

*I.*—Something better? Have you forgotten what Lamartine said about him? He called Béranger: "the fiddler every stroke of whose bow is drawn across the heart-strings of thirty-six million people, moving them to pity or exaltation." That was more than could be said for Hugo, or for Lamartine.

*HE.*—Béranger was only a ballad-maker.

*I.*—Yes, and the one form of verse that really appeals to the masses is the ballad made to be sung. Don't look down your nose at popular ballads. It is true that when

Béranger wrote them they were always wingless and almost always vulgar; it hurts us to think that his songs used to be praised as the voice of the French people. To our shame be it said that his vulgarity was what allowed him to pass for a "national poet." But many of our old ballads, especially those by unknown authors, are delightful; and moreover they speak in the real voice of France, which is cautious and at the same time bold, ardent; which sometimes has solemn tones, but is by preference cheerful, given to mockery and gently ironic even in its tenderness. Apollinaire tended toward the ballad, as Aragon sometimes does today. We must remember, however, that real poetry, at least till the present time, has always been the expression of private personalities that addressed themselves, not to the public at large, but to individual readers. Popularity is achieved only at the cost of being commonplace. Let us quickly add: in literature.

*HE.*—Let us also add: in France. For we know that the English people enjoy Shakespeare; the Russian people, Pushkin and Tolstoy; the Spanish people, Cervantes. German villagers know by heart the *Lieder* of Goethe and Schiller; and I was promised, if I went to Tuscany, that I should hear Dante's verses recited by simple peasants.

*I.*—O happy nations and happy poets! Yes, France has always been the country of individualism. Thierry-Maulnier has made some judicious remarks on that subject, in his copious *Introduction à la poésie française*. Won't you take the book, there on my table, and read me the passages I have underlined? They will help to clarify

your ideas and will, it seems to me, give us a better idea
of what we are talking about.

The book opened of its own accord to page 39, and
he read:

"The French people have a culture that is among the
oldest in the world, but French writers ask nothing of
the people and do not write for them. In the history of
French literature there has never been anything an-
alogous to the Greek epic, the Greek theater, the Spanish *romancero*, the Elizabethan drama, or the German
poetry that is diffused through the German soul and
mingled with German daily life, to such a point that it inspires the composers, directs and gives a cadence to
marching youth, and shapes the political movements."

*HE.*—Yes, in better terms, that is what I was saying
a moment ago.

*I.*—And therefore you take it as gospel. But listen
to these two brief quotations that I jotted down long
before the war. The first is from Fénelon, and I found it
in his *Letter to the Academy*, written a year before his
death in 1715. In offering his advice to poets, and just
after reproaching Ronsard for having "violated our language with inversions that were too daring and obscure,"
he said: "It is time to stop short when one sees that one
is no longer being followed by the multitude"; and then
he added: "Singularity is dangerous in everything."

It seems to me that the second text reveals the ideas
that minds without great scope, but subtle, shrewd, and
of considerable learning, were disposed to hold in the
seventeenth century. It comes from Chapelain, who was
known in his time as "the lawgiver of Parnassus"; and I

found it in a letter he addressed to Guez de Balzac in May 1640—a letter that remained unpublished until Sainte-Beuve quoted it in the course of an article on Ronsard included in Volume XII of his *Mondays.* Chapelain set out to attack Ronsard in almost the same terms that Fénelon would use seventy-four years later, condemning him for his indiscreet imitation of the classics and for introducing into our language a quantity of terms derived from the Greek, a bevy of gods and goddesses whose names seemed like learned claptrap to "*the people, for whom poetry is written.*" He used the last phrase without emphasis, not as if he were advancing a boldly personal opinion that he was getting ready to defend, but as a quite simple truth, current and recognized. So you can see that the subject with which you are preoccupied is not merely a question of the day.

*HE.*—I confess to being surprised by these opinions of Fénelon and Chapelain. In other words, the literature of our great classical century, which has often been censured for being too refined, for having stood aside from real life, and for having concerned itself merely with the somewhat artificial life of leisured people in good society who were protected from all preoccupations other than those of the heart and the mind . . .

*I.*—That literature, as you see, was already worried about answering the needs of the great public, and believed that it had answered them; and also believed that writers were taking the wrong road when they ceased to be "followed by the multitude."

*HE.*—How do you explain that illusion?—for plainly there is nothing else it could be.

*I.*—Don't you find that my two quotations are rather instructive? But I hardly think that they justify sweeping conclusions. It would be more reasonable to say that the words "people" and "multitude" included only those whom Molière called *les honnêtes gens,* the gentlefolk; in other words, very few persons as compared with the enormous mass of those who weren't even regarded as people; who were busy cultivating our fields and therefore remained outside the domain of Culture.

*HE.*—So Thierry-Maulnier was right after all?

*I.*—But when he adds—just pass me the book: "In France, poetry does not attain to incandescence or to its true dimensions except in the sanctuary of a strange silence; it becomes more profound by withdrawing from the world; its brightest lightning flashes are always characterized by something secret, unwonted, and wild" —then we see that even in the seventeenth century there was no lack of sensible men to protest against the tendency he admires, which has always been evident in our literature: I shall not say the tendency toward the esoteric, but the tendency to become excessively intellectual and to draw apart from life. Thierry-Maulnier describes it very well. "French poetry," he says, "distrusts all raw material and prefers not to welcome objects, beings, or sentiments until they have been perfected and ennobled by a long cohabitation with literature."

*HE.*—But doesn't it happen now and again, beginning with Villon, or even earlier with Rutebeuf, that a simple and essentially human emotion comes to the surface and finds its musical expression in a direct fashion, without undergoing that process of distillation in the mind?

*I.*—We are forced to recognize that these "now and agains" are somewhat rare, at least until the Romantic period. They are so rare, indeed, that Thierry-Maulnier can be forgiven for overlooking them completely; he may well have been embarrassed by poems that ran counter to his thesis; or again he may have no ear for what is purely music and emotion. In any case, what he most enjoys and praises is everything farthest removed from the natural and spontaneous. Listen: there are two exquisite verses by Maurice Scève for which I should gladly sacrifice all the remaining intricacies of his *Délie.* You know them, I suppose:

> *Toute douceur d'amour est détrempée*
> *De fiel amer et de mortel venin*

—"Everything sweet in love is interfused, With bitter gall and mortal venom." Well, you would seek in vain for those two lines among the 280 from *Délie* that are reprinted in Thierry-Maulnier's anthology. He prefers and asks us to admire:

> *Tout jugement de celle infinité,*
> *Où tout concept se trouve superflus,*
> *Et tout aigu de perspicuité*
> *Ne pourroyent joindre au sommet de son plus.*
> *Car seulement l'apparent du surplus . . .*[1]

—line after line in the same alembicated style.

---

[1] Scève at his worst—as in these lines, which it would be pointless to translate—is like the worst of the English metaphysical poets.—Tr.

*HE.*—I begin to understand why there is not a verse from Verlaine or Moréas or Jammes in his anthology.

*I.*—And also the reason for his rejection of the whole Romantic movement. I think it is less a matter of injustice than of insensitivity. Until he came to the Romantics, he was perhaps right to say—and he says it very well indeed—"In France, subjects taken from life or history, before entering the magic ring where they will undergo their final combustion, must first pass through a preliminary stage or term of probation in literature that raises them to the dignity of themes." But you doubt whether he ever read the *Expiation* when a moment later you find him making bold to declare: "Napoleon merely inspires Hugo to unbearable declamations." The truth is that Hugo, in spite of his bombast, speaks of things directly; and perhaps that is the salient characteristic of Romanticism as a whole. But it is also what Thierry-Maulnier cannot tolerate. What he loves, the only poetry he understands, is poetry that has been twice refined. Undoubtedly this poetry, which is specially and specifically French, has sometimes shone with incomparable brilliance. Apollo be praised, it is not the only poetry. For the French there are always, in every field (and so much the better), two poles, two tendencies, two parties; in our own field there is, on the one side, reflective poetry (I am using the word in its two senses of "contemplative" and "reflected as in a mirror"), and on the other side, direct poetry; Oronte's sonnet as against the "Ballad of King Henry." [2] I confess that

[2] This refers to the famous scene in Act I of Molière's *The Misanthrope* where Oronte reads a sonnet in the affected style of the time

I don't find the sonnet so absurd and that I come close
to preferring:

> *L'Espoir, il est vrai, nous soulage*
> *Et nous berce un temps notre ennui . . .*

> Hope, it is true, will solace us,
> And cradle our dejection for a day,

to:

> *Si le roi m'avoit donné*
> *Paris sa grand'ville,*
> *Et qu'il me fallût quitter*
> *L'amour de ma mie . . .*

> If the King had given me
> Paris, his great city,
> And for that I had to leave
> The arms of my pretty,

which, be it said between us, is nothing much. Still, for all
the splendors of cerebral poetry in France, it is from the
other tendency, from direct poetry, that I am now expecting our renaissance: from the mood that inspired
Aragon to write the poems in *Heartbreak*—Aragon,
whose first stories filled us with admiration, whose later
books down to the war gave us less pleasure, or none at
all, and sometimes even dumbfounded us, so that we
began to fear he was forever lost to literature. But of his
own accord he has doubtless recognized his error. Yes,
he is coming back from a long journey when, scarcely

---

and Alceste tells him that he prefers the simple "Ballad of King
Henry."—Tr.

dry from the sweat of battle, he gives us lines of as good
alloy as these (and I might have quoted many others) :

> Hour after hour, without relief
> I sought a half-remembered grief
> Until the September dawn
>
> When lying in your arms awake
> I heard one singing at daybreak
> Outside, an old French song
> Then knew my sorrow, branch and root
> Its music like a naked foot
> Troubled the pool where silence lay nightlong.[3]

And now, by the way, I suppose you will take a vacation?

*HE.*—Oh, the truth is, I hardly . . .

*I.*—Then I'll take one instead. When I get back, I'll
let you know.

---

[3] These are the last nine lines of Aragon's now famous poem, "Zone
Libre." They read, in the original:

> *Je cherchais à n'en plus finir*
> *Cette douleur sans souvenir*
> *Quand parut l'aube de septembre.*
>
> *Mon amour j'étais dans tes bras*
> *Au dehors quelqu'un murmura*
> *Une vieille chanson de France*
> *Mon mal enfin s'est reconnu*
> *Et son refrain comme un pied nu*
> *Troubla l'eau verte du silence.*

# IMAGINARY INTERVIEW · 7

HAVING put off my vacation indefinitely, I let him know. He came back.

"Please don't insist," I said to him when he began plying me with questions about current—and therefore untimely—matters. "There are many things it is better not to talk about today. Of one thing I am certain: literary subjects are all I can discuss with you. And I won't change my mind, even if I have to disappoint your readers; you can warn them."

*HE.*—Chardonne's last book, *Voir la Figure,* comes under the heading of literature; nevertheless it is alive with topical interest.

*I.*—Yes, but it veers with the wind.

*HE.*—Would you be willing to discuss it?

*I.*—I read it with keen interest. Certainly this new book deserves none of the criticisms I made of the one that preceded it; [1] and that is what gave Chardonne the

---

[1] His *Chronique Privée de l'An 1940,* a collaborationist work that Gide condemned as bad thinking and bad art. See the chapter "Chardonne 1940," pp. 147–54.—Tr.

idea of reprinting my review in the appendix to *Voir la
Figure;* since the criticism is no longer merited, it seems
unjustified. It had plenty of justification in its time.
But without losing the virtues of his excellent style,
Chardonne has confirmed himself in—

*HE.*—Apparently your article acted on him like one
of those chemical agents that form what is called a pre-
cipitate.

*I.*—His position is now the same as that of Renan
when he wrote his letter to Strauss, shortly after our defeat in 1870.

*HE.*—In his *Intellectual and Moral Reform*, Renan
reprints two letters to Strauss.

*I.*—Chardonne confines himself to the first.[2]

*HE.*—He is younger than you. Surely the indecision
for which you condemned him came from the fact that
he was then passing through a period of perplexity,
doubts, and self-examination—in which you still linger,
perhaps, but from which you see that he has now
emerged.

*I.*—Perhaps not completely; for he confesses that he
has been "plagued" by a statement from that same letter
of Renan's. Well, Chardonne knows his French and he
chose exactly the right word. The statement to which

---

2 Renan's first open letter to David Friedrich Strauss, author of *Das
Leben Jesu,* was published in September 1870. It was friendly toward
the Germans and even conciliatory, but not "collaborationist" in the
present sense of the word. Gide, however, doesn't want his readers
to miss the second letter. Published a year later, after the Prussian
army had marched through Paris, it was defiant toward Germany
and full of highly polished insults directed toward Strauss himself
as a representative of the German scholars who had supported the
war.—Tr.

he referred—I can't quote it exactly—was concerned with the great dangers incurred by morality and intelligence in a certain state of humanity.

*HE.*—No doubt the dangers are all the greater because, as you said the other day, they are "imperceptible"; or at least there are now very few minds capable of perceiving them.

*I.*—And still fewer minds that have the courage, the wisdom, or the ability to name them. So it is that silence has closed over dying civilizations.

*HE.*—Long live our National Revolution, which preserves us from such a fate! It permits us to wish and hope for a general reconciliation.

There was a moment of silence.

He began again: "Chardonne's book also reprints in the appendix the diatribe against you by Martin du Gard."

*I.*—Martin du Gard! You mean Maurice Martin du Gard, the journalist, who is no relation to the great writer.

*HE.*—Yes, it was Maurice. Excuse me.

*I.*—That was the article in which you find the noble phrase: "Old Narcissus"—I think he refers to me— "leans over the murky waters of opportunism, his ears strained to hear the drunken whispers of the champions of the gold standard"; not to mention other amenities. What can you expect? People write as they think. Still it is curious, this mania for ascribing vile motives to those who hold opinions one doesn't share. Let us have done with Maurice, if you please, and get back to literature.

Last Saturday we were talking about folk literature, but only about poetry. Besides its charming *Lieder*, we are indebted to German folklore for a great number of *Märchen*. The brothers Grimm, as you know, made a huge collection of fairy stories, a very precious volume that has often been a companion of my travels. If only I had taken it with me this time!

*HE.*—Haven't we Perrault's fairy tales?

*I.*—Set beside Grimm, they cut almost too fine a figure; they seem studied, remote from the peasants who created them, polished, raked like a formal garden. The German tales, though sometimes formless by comparison, are almost always sturdy, sanguine, not burdened with intellectuality, but with life. There are tender and charming *Märchen*, like "Marienkind," an Occidental and Christian echo of the story told by one of the Kalandars in the *Thousand and One Nights*. It was in Grimm that Maeterlinck found the germ of his *Princesse Maleine*. There are also brutal and cynical *Märchen*, and I find them no less savory.

*HE.*—In France we know only the happy stories, translated for children.

*I.*—And more's the pity. I remember one that bears the title . . . "Herr Korbes," I believe. It is a very brief story: a cat, a cobblestone, an egg, a duck, a pin, and a needle all happened to meet. "Isn't it nice," they said, "we can go to see Herr Korbes." He wasn't home from work when they arrived, so they settled down to wait for him. The cat curled up on the hearth, the duck climbed into the hand basin, the egg rolled itself into a towel, the pin stuck itself into the chair cushion, the needle jumped up on the bed and lay down on the pillow, and the cobble-stone perched on the lintel of the door. When Herr Korbes came home and went to the hearth, the cat threw ashes in his face. He tried to wash, but the duck flapped its wings and splashed water over him. He started to dry himself with the towel, but the egg broke in his eyes and blinded him. He sat down in the chair and the pin pricked him. He threw himself on the bed and the needle scratched his face, so that he screamed in pain and started to run out the door, but the cobblestone fell on him and crushed his head. And the story ends: "Herr Korbes must have been a very wicked man."

*HE.*—The story seems just as stupid as your fable from the Congo. It makes me think of that passage from *Alice in Wonderland* where people are condemned before they are tried, after which it only remains to commit the crime. Quite simply it is putting the cart before the horse. I don't find that very funny.

*I.*—Nor do I. But there are people who laugh at it. In France we lack humor. The greatest difference between one nation and another is in their jokes.

I had risen from my chair.

*HE.*—Before I go, would you let me return to a subject we mentioned before? I am not sure that I quite understood the nature of the dangers that Renan mentioned.

*I.*—What dangers?

*HE.*—Those to which he thinks that intelligence and morality would be exposed as the result of a general reconciliation. Isn't such a reconciliation the goal we are hoping to reach?

*I.*—It is a pity that you don't see the dangers, for it isn't my task to explain what they are.

I hastily said good-by, for fear of having to confess that I too was unable to visualize them clearly. After he had gone, I remained in a thoughtful mood; and even in bed that night I continued to repeat: "Happiness! The best in man! The greatest number! . . . To sacrifice the best in man to obtain the happiness of the greatest number!"

And I fell asleep in much the same fashion that the individual is absorbed into the mass, sinking into a slumber full of unconsciousness and irresponsibility.

# IMAGINARY INTERVIEW · 8

"I HAVE brought you a Paris weekly," he said. "It has a piece about you by your friend Léautaud."

*I.*—You frighten me.

*HE.*—There's nothing to be disturbed about. It's just that Léautaud is surprised because, when you were asked by an American magazine to name the twelve books you would take along to a desert island, your list included nothing but novels.

*I.*—Léautaud is mistaken.[1] It was a French, not an American, magazine that asked the question, and my choice was strictly limited. I was to name the twelve French novels I preferred; or rather the twelve I regarded as landmarks in the history of our literature. I answered with comments to explain my choice, and these were perhaps reprinted in the United States; at any rate, they were included in one of my critical volumes. If I were forced by some disaster to save only twelve books out of

---

1 Paul Léautaud is an elderly critic known for his sharp tongue and his fondness for cats. The list, which is twenty years old, included ten novels, not twelve. For their titles, see the Appendix, "Ten Desert-Island Novels."—Tr.

my library, there would not be a single novel among those that remained. Still, I might keep *War and Peace*, for the subtle reason that, in spite of many efforts, I never found pleasure or even took real interest in that great work, and I don't want to stop trying.

*HE.*—At least you have read it.

*I.*—From cover to cover, when I was young. At present I am talking about books to reread. Tolstoy has an incomparable power of evocation; but this succession of historical panoramas (I am thinking only of *War and Peace*) where everything is equally lighted; where there are no shadows, no relief, no chiaroscuro, no art, soon plunges me into a state of lassitude. It is a confession I am making, a somewhat hesitant confession; but although it may be the wisest policy, in one's youth, to strain one's power of admiration without being too much worried about one's personal tastes; to learn to enjoy what deserves to be enjoyed, and perhaps wouldn't be liked at all if the reader followed his natural bent; still it can't be a mistake, when one has reached my age, to be perfectly candid with oneself and others by saying: "No, with everything considered and reconsidered, that isn't my type of book"—then try to explain the reasons why.

*HE.*—It is a way of justifying one's early tastes, which had begun by being quite spontaneous.

*I.*—No; or at least it is more than that. The early tastes, by patient study and comparison, have been strengthened, broadened, clarified; and it is not unlikely that they have changed. I am a Stendhal enthusiast to-day; but at first I had to make an effort to like him. He used to seem dry to me; I was wrong. But if I had to

make my choice among Stendhal's works, I am convinced
that I should abandon his novels sooner than leave behind his *Memoirs of an Egotist,* his correspondence, or
his *Life of Henri Brulard.* The stories he tells in *The
Charterhouse of Parma* and *The Red and the Black*
interest me less than his fashion of telling them, less
than the author himself. The more he reveals himself,
the better I like him. For the same reasons, I should
choose Flaubert's letters rather than his novels.

*HE.*—In short, you regard the novel as of secondary
importance?

*I.*—Not at all. And Flaubert's letters would interest
me much less if Flaubert weren't the author of *Senti-
mental Education* and *Salammbô.* But I am something
of a botanist and look at the plant to find the explana-
tion of the flower. I have a tendency (perhaps it is a
fault) to be more interested in the producer than in the
product, just as Valéry is more interested in the "recipe"
that the artist followed.

*HE.*—Would you have the same feeling about Racine's
letters to Boileau as compared with his tragedies?

*I.*—Perhaps, if the letters were more numerous and
less reserved ; if he used them as an opportunity for discussing his work and his technical problems, like Flaubert, instead of bowing and scraping like the courtiers
of his time. . . . But on second thought, no, not even
then. Not even for the privilege of penetrating into the
secrets of his art, of understanding how, why, and after
overcoming what difficulties he was able to achieve perfection in his tragedies, would I sacrifice the pure joy
I feel each time I reread them.

*HE.*—So Racine's dramatic works would be among the twelve books you would keep?

*I.*—Most certainly. I never grow tired of them, whereas I should soon grow tired of a novel, even if it were the one perfect novel in the world.

*HE.*—Did you mean to say "perfect novel"?

*I.*—It was a slip of the tongue and you were right to catch me up. The word "perfect" is particularly inappropriate when applied to a novel. Logically it cannot be applied except to an object or work of art that must obey definite laws. The novel is a form with such vague outlines that it cannot aspire to perfection.

*HE.*—You would then agree that what Kléber Haedens says in his *Paradox on the Novel* is essentially correct?

*I.*—Correct and well expressed, but not very important. The artificial rules against which he protests have hardly been a great burden to the novelists of our own time. Haedens is right to say that conforming to the rules doesn't make a second-rate novelist any better. On the other hand, it wouldn't be hard to demonstrate that many of the great novelists paid no attention to the rules, which have ceased to exist or which survive only in the backward minds of certain critics.

*HE.*—But I remember that when Edmond Jaloux, the least backward of the critics, presented *Madame Bovary* as a model and pattern, he gave us to understand that Flaubert had subjected himself to what he regarded as the laws of the novel.

*I.*—But the laws weren't pre-established; it was Flaubert who created them and imposed them on himself

while composing his book; and he was ready to defy
them when writing *The Temptation of St. Anthony* or
*Bouvard and Pécuchet.* Goethe likewise, without ever
formulating them precisely, confined himself to strict
rules for each of his important works; but those rules
were inherent in the work itself and varied according to
its nature, each work being the answer to a particular
and special summons of his genius. *Götz von Berlichin-
gen* is a finished work in its own medium; so too are
*Torquato Tasso, Iphigenia, The Elective Affinities,* and
the first *Faust,* in their very different mediums. As for
*Wilhelm Meister* and the second *Faust,* if the word "finished" seems inappropriate when applied to them, it is
because these two works are in a medium that admits of
an infinite fluctuation.

*HE.*—Might it not be said that the only works observing the precise laws of a form or genre are those in
which a certain limitation of time is imposed on the
author? Such is the case with the oratorical form; and
for this reason Bossuet's *Funeral Orations* and some
of his sermons impress us as being exemplary. Such also
is the case with all dramatic works; they must not ex-
ceed the time that people allot to theater-going, which
is not the same in all countries. Spanish plays are per-
ceptibly shorter than our classical tragedies, which in
turn lack the elbow room that Wagner gave to his music
dramas. All three, however, answer an expectation, a
demand by the public. Claudel's dramas in verse answer
a demand that has still to be made, a need that he hopes
to create in the public at large, but one that has existed
only sporadically until now, and in certain individuals.

Hence the difficulties encountered in producing his works on the stage.

*I.*—Everything you say seems accurate. Moreover, I feel that the short story has gained the right to be called a genre chiefly because it is limited to the space available in newspapers and magazines. It is written to be read at one sitting. As soon as there is a "to be continued," as soon as the reader is left in suspense, it is encroaching on the genre "novel"—which is not a genre, strictly speaking, because it has no laws of its own.

*HE.*—So that the word "perfect," which seems out of place with a novel, might be applied to a short story.

*I.*—In any case it would seem less inappropriate; and I am ready to use it when speaking, for example, of Pushkin's "The Shot" and "The Queen of Spades," two masterpieces of their kind; of Maupassant's *Boule de Suif* and—

*HE.*—Excuse me. *Boule de Suif* couldn't be printed in one issue of a magazine.

*I.*—I was playing your cards; you might have let me cheat a little. But it's getting late, and we can come back to this subject after the new year begins. Let us hope that it will be less dismal than these two wretched years of disgrace.

*HE.*—Fortunately a few gleams of light are beginning to appear.

*I.*—In a tunnel artificial lighting serves as best it can. Before seeing daylight, I am afraid we shall have to plunge deeper into the shadows. Meanwhile, let us cling to hope.

# IMAGINARY INTERVIEW · 9

"What you said last week about the novel," I told him, "not only impressed me as being true but set me to thinking that works intended for an audience, for a group of people brought together for a definite time, are the only ones capable of constituting what I have called a genre. And if novels lack the strict rules that would make them a genre, I wonder whether it isn't chiefly because they are addressed to separate individuals, as poems are likewise. The task of a novel is to persuade or impress, to retain the charmed attention—but of a reader who takes his own time, lending himself to the game only when he feels so inclined; and this, I should say, explains why the game has no rules that the author is forced to observe. Before books had become a commodity, in the old days of rhapsodies, bards, minstrels, and public recitations, epic poetry could be called a genre, as could our *chansons de gestes*. But there is no good reason why the novel I read when sitting alone in my comfortable chair, at the moments that best suit my leisure, should bother itself with rules that the reader doesn't expect it to follow.

"The case is different when one reads a book aloud in the family circle, as I often used to do in my younger days. At such times the divagations of genius, the tedious expositions and sublime irrelevancies, seem out of place; and the chosen author must answer the expectations and desires of several persons at once. As a result of reading aloud to a group that included persons of different ages and sexes, all of whom were equally attentive and quite intelligent, I came to perceive rather clearly what the rules of the novel would be if it ever became a genre; and they are good rules too, in spite of Kléber Haedens. Nevertheless, when I had retired to my own room, they didn't keep me from greatly enjoying and admiring some pseudo-novel of genius that broke all the rules—whether the book was *Tristram Shandy, Pantagruel, Dead Souls, Green Heinrich, Marius the Epicurean,* or *Remembrance of Things Past.*"

*HE.*—The genre is addressed to a group; the novel is addressed to individuals. Is that the distinction?

*I.*—Yes; and after what we have just said, it is interesting to note that the novel as a topic for discussion is closely related to the question of individualism. Nations rich in novels are also nations in which the individual is most clearly distinguished, and tries hardest to distinguish himself, from the mass. *Par contre*, the form in which Germany excels and triumphs is the lyrical drama, a synthetic form in which music and poetry collaborate toward a total effect. This form, which achieved its flowering in Wagner's *Ring*, is one to which an assembled throng listens religiously, and in which, I should judge, the great social fusion of our time can recognize its most appropriate expression.

*HE.*—You suggest that countries where the novel is at home are also countries marked by individualism; and yet the Russian novel—

*I.*—At first glance I seem to have been on the wrong track. Still, after a little reflection it occurs to me that in Russia under the czars there was little chance of assembling those vast audiences for which Dostoyevsky might have written the dramas he talked about in his early letters to his brother. He abandoned the project, knowing as he did that he would have to address each of his readers separately.

*HE.*—And we might add that the Russian novel has evolved since then, either by inner compulsion or, more likely, as a result of social upheavals; it has become, so to speak, disindividualized. It now seeks the support of whole communities. Crusoe is never alone in Russia; he is a group of pioneers.

We were silent for a few moments; then, after he had caught his breath, "Doubtless," he said, "you were thinking chiefly about England when you mentioned countries that are rich in novels. And yet the Elizabethan dramatists—"

*I.*—What a lot of questions you raise! But I'm not defending a thesis.

*HE.*—This particular question might end by confirming your thesis. In England the dramatists preceded the novelists. The theater flourished in those early days when the people were still united. When the novel appeared, with *Paradise Lost*, it was after the revolts and religious dissensions brought about by the Reformation, which was the mother of individualism. Cromwell closed the theaters, dispersed the spectators, sundered the mass into individuals. Milton's poem speaks to each of those individuals separately, and that is why I described it as a novel: nothing could be less suitable for great throngs; nothing is better designed for reading alone in one's study . . . or so it seems to me. What is your opinion on the subject?

*I.*—As yet I haven't any, in all likelihood. I have to think it over. It wouldn't be the first time I found there was more reason on my side than I had at first believed. In any case, I thank you for agreeing with me.

*HE.*—Your smile gives me courage to mention something else. A little while ago you said *par contre*, "by opposition."

*I.*—I realize that both Voltaire and Littré forbid us to use the expression, and that Littré advises *en revanche* or *en compensation*,[2] but it hardly seems to me that these two phrases are always appropriate; and they would be singularly out of place in the sentence where you noted my *par contre*—not to mention all the other statements to which one could add the word "alas!" Would you think it proper for a woman to say: "Yes, my brother and my husband came back safe from the war, but *in revenge* I lost my two sons"?—or would a farmer tell

---

[2] "In revenge," "as compensation," and "by opposition" are three expressions roughly equivalent to the English "on the other hand." But note the examples from life that Gide offers in support of his grammatical distinctions. Here and elsewhere his real subject is the grammar of resistance.—Tr.

you: "The yield of grain wasn't bad this year, but *as compensation* our potatoes rotted in the ground"?

*HE.*—All we have to do is turn the sentence around and keep the best for the last: "Our potatoes rotted in the ground, but *as compensation* the yield of grain wasn't bad." We lose nothing from the fact that the language itself forces the French to look at the world from a cheerful point of view.

*I.*—But sometimes the language plays tricks on us. These days it hardly seems to me that "in revenge" is the right phrase to use. Even "in compensation" can find no lodging in my heart or mind. I need "by opposition," and, with all respect to Littré, I propose to keep it.

He had risen to go when something else occurred to him. "Did you read the issue of *Le Figaro*," he said, "that contained Thierry-Maulnier's remarks on our discussion about poetry?"

*I.*—Of course I did, and I was grateful to him for his courtesy. A debate of this sort can be extremely profitable, so long as neither of the debaters tries to wound or humiliate the other. Thierry-Maulnier's arguments reassured me by their fairness; they lead to reflection rather than personal combat. Although he and I find different sorts of pleasure and different magics in poetry, we nevertheless come together at certain points: those where ideas are expressed in such fine verse that they become musical, and those where the music of the verse is impregnated with ideas. Such points of confluence are not so rare that the two of us must remain strangers. But we should come to an undertsanding about the word "music," which might otherwise throw us off on the

wrong scent. The word should be defined so that it would
no longer be possible for Thierry-Maulnier to think and
say: "If you want music, you should go to the concert
hall." The musical quality of a poem has nothing to do
with music properly speaking, which is based on a scale
of notes ; and nothing in common with singing. What I
call music, in this connection, is the alliance of meter
and tonal quality, of emotion and thought, that exists
to such a high degree in one of Valéry's shorter poems
that I cannot refrain from quoting it (but in its first
version, which I prefer to the one he later published) :

> *O courbes, méandre,*
> *Secret du menteur,*
> *Est-il art plus tendre*
> *Que cette lenteur?*
>
> *Je sais où je vais,*
> *Laisse-toi conduire,*
> *Mon dessein mauvais*
> *N'est pas de te nuire . . .*
>
> *Bien que souriante*
> *En toute fierté*
> *Tant de liberté*
> *Te désoriente?*
>
> *O courbes, méandre,*
> *Secret du menteur,*
> *Je veux faire attendre*
> *Le mot le plus tendre.*[3]

[3] Since Gide quotes this fine poem for its music, exactly the quality
that would be lost in even the best translation, I have let it stand in
the original.—Tr.

*HE.*—I see what you mean. And here is another example: among the few lines from Hugo that have found grace with Thierry-Maulnier, I was delighted to recognize the superb alexandrine:

> *O Seigneur! ouvrez-moi les portes de la nuit*

—"Throw open, Lord, the portals of the night"; but a moment later I was chagrined to find that Thierry-Maulnier had divorced it from the following line:

> *Afin que je m'en aille et que je disparaisse*

—"Let me depart and let me disappear"—a line which echoes with the same grave music and without which the other verse, so it seems to me, stops halfway in its perfect curve.

*I.*—Yes, you are right. And I hope that Thierry-Maulnier won't say, in this connection, that the second verb is redundant; it is nothing of the sort. "To depart," for Hugo, is something less than "to disappear." The departing star leaves trails of glory behind it. "And let me disappear" is tragic in its beauty.

*HE.*—Is it not this musical quality that we cherish in the poetry of Racine and seldom find in even the finest lines from Corneille?

*I.*—And what could be more musical than the few lines from Hugo's *Legend of the Ages* that follow the commonplace and famous song of Eviradnus:

> *La mélodie encor quelques instants se traîne*
> *Sous les arbres bleus par la lune sereine*
> *Puis tremble, puis expire, et la voix qui chantait*
> *S'éteint comme un oiseau se pose; tout se tait.*

A moment still the melody is strewn
Under the trees blue-shadowed by the moon;
It trembles, then expires. The voice that trilled
Now dies as birds sink earthward. All is stilled.

*HE.*—What could be less musical, *par contre*, than
Musset's lines:

> *Harmonie! Harmonie!*
> *Langue que pour l'amour inventa le génie,*
> *Qui nous vint d'Italie et qui lui vint des cieux!*

—"Harmony, harmony, language invented for love by
genius, which came to us from Italy and came to genius
from the skies." The lines are rendered all the more discordant by the fact that music is the subject with which
they deal.

*I.*—Having almost no books at hand, I have quoted
from memory. I hope your readers will excuse me if I
have made a few errors.

# IMAGINARY INTERVIEW · 10

I TOLD him that I had been surprised by some of the remarks he made during his last visit.

*HE.*—I hardly think I said anything that you weren't on the point of saying yourself.

*I.*—Perhaps; but you said it first.

*HE.*—I have been gaining more assurance as I mastered my trade. The interview is a sort of Socratic dialogue. In order to act as midwife to your thoughts, I agree or contradict as seems more desirable.

*I.*—Recently you have done almost nothing but agree.

*HE.*—When talking with you, I try to be self-effacing; I regard myself as a mirror. I go so far as to imitate your fashion of speaking, your turns of phrase—oh, without meaning to do so; it becomes an occupational disease. As soon as I am alone, I step back into my own character, much as an actor does when he walks off the stage. But the actor, when he takes off the costume of a stage hero, returns to himself as if falling from a height; whereas I, whom you seem to regard as just good enough to ask questions and write down your answers—

Since I happened to be rich in tobacco, as the result

of some friendly gifts, I invited him to fill his pipe and
talk.

*HE.*—Let me begin by telling you that I'm not the
person you think. No, I'm his younger brother. It's
curious how little attention you pay to people's ages.
Ramon Fernandez was right to say that you lack the
historical sense. The interviewer who came to see you
twice in 1905 was much younger than you, but still he
was my senior by twenty years; in fact, I had just been
born. They tell me that I resemble him; or rather that
now, at thirty-six, I resemble what he was then and what
for many years he has ceased to be. I'm sure you wouldn't
recognize him today.

He took a few deep puffs at his pipe; and then in a
great burst of frankness, "Would you like to know who
I am?" he said. "Perhaps I am that hundred and first
or second author on whom you based the poetic future
of France."

*I.*—A poet?

*HE.*—And I trembled with hope the other day when
I heard you reserving the future for the man who could
wait. What else have I done but wait and reflect and
ripen in silence? But I feel that I shan't be able to hold
my silence much longer.

*I.*—A poet-poet?

*HE.*—I would rather say a novelist-poet. Precisely
of the type that Kléber Haedens advocates. Yes, I wholly
agreed with you when you said that the novel could not be
regarded as a genre because it had no laws of its own;
and that it had no laws because it was addressed to each
reader separately. But why not take advantage of all

the boundless liberties you granted to this synthetic form? There is more to be done with it, much more, than anyone has attempted in the past.

Now he was launched. I had only to sit back and let him talk.

*HE.*—"To compete with the town clerk's records": what a silly program for Balzac to have undertaken! The function of art is by no means that of a mirror. A character like César Birotteau would have no interest for us if we met him in life; and the mere image of a Birotteau would not deserve to hold our attention. Balzac's painting of him concerns us only in so far as it deserts the model, only in so far as Balzac sacrifices the man to his art. Art begins at the point where we liberate ourselves from nature. What we have to learn is that the artist can handle forms and colors as he pleases; but this is a fact he is only beginning to realize. I propose, as a novelist, to pay no attention to reality; to be like the painter who, after placing one value on his canvas, places beside it another value that gives him pleasure, without caring whether or not it is copied from nature. A violet sea under an orange-tinted sky, for example; or vice versa. In the same way, Lautréamont was not afraid to talk about the "ruby" of champagne.

*I.*—I should advise your painter not to change his colors too much unless they belong to objects that are at least recognizable by their forms. A sky or a sea without any outlines does not seem to me well chosen for this particular exercise. The spectator simply won't understand.

On the moment, however, I regretted my sententious

remark. I could read contempt in the look he gave me as he exclaimed that we could never understand each other and that assuredly there was a gulf between us. Now, I have a particular horror of gulfs. I felt myself capable of understanding my interviewer even when he thought we were farthest apart. Moreover, the ideas he expressed seemed to me less novel than confused, and the gulf between us imaginary. I began again in a more conciliatory tone, as though building a footbridge.

*I.*—Look, here is a small canvas by Derain that I think is enchanting. I can see that it represents or suggests a beach with a wave curling over it, a cliff, and a smoke-colored sky. What explains, I wonder, the potent and inescapable charm of the picture? The color? The weight of these forms? The highly personal quality of the handling and the subject? The air is unbreathable and the sea unnavigable; no one would ever venture on that beach. If nature offered such a scene, you would be overcome with horror. And yet . . . And yet there is some connection with our own sky, with a real cliff and the real sea; otherwise the picture would lose its reason for being, its composition, its life.

*HE.*—But its power of seduction is due precisely to the extraordinary distance between the object evoked and the painting that evokes it.

*I.*—Yes, and to the imaginative force that surmounts the distance. A little less distance and we should cease to be charmed; a little more and the charm would be broken. It would be inexistent if the picture came too close to reality; broken if it ceased to evoke reality. I think that the case is the same with the novelist. He can dispose of his materials as he sees fit, but they are the materials proposed by nature. You cannot do without them.

He listened a little impatiently and, as soon as I paused, he resumed his earlier chain of thought, as if closing a parenthesis around my remarks.

*HE.*—I think that what keeps the novel in leading-strings is not its attachment to ancient rules, for these are no longer observed, but rather (and this will make you start) its insistence on depicting characters.

*I.*—Merely to tell me that something will make me start is enough to keep me from starting. But don't stop there: are you going to do without characters?

*HE.*—No; but I shan't grow attached to them; I shan't follow their adventures. What I should like to follow is the effect, on characters chosen at random and quickly abandoned, of a phrase or a deed. . . . You are willing to admit, I suppose, that a casually uttered phrase sometimes has tragic effects on the lives of those who chance to overhear it. Take for example: "Great Pan is dead." It doesn't matter who is the first to spread this terrifying news; it passes from mouth to mouth, changing everything as it goes, and nothing can stop it.

*I.*—I begin to see what you are driving at. No doubt you have read one of Browning's most curious and ingenious poems, *Pippa Passes?* A little Florentine silk-weaver goes through the streets singing; and her songs, as she wanders on her way, are overheard by one person after another who has no connection with Pippa, but whose life will be profoundly changed from that moment by the words that Pippa sings. They bring about or put an end to tragic situations; they cause young men to enter new careers of heroism or art. Pippa herself merely passes; she is the unconscious and involuntary agent of destiny. Nevertheless she holds our interest except when it is momentarily transferred to the chance persons who overhear her song. You must attach the reader's interest to someone or something, or else it will bid you farewell. On what do you propose to center your action?

*HE.*—When did I speak of action? A phrase or a word is enough, I tell you. For another example, there is Galileo's *Eppur si muove*. What could be more important, more tragic? It was the expression of a hitherto unrecognized truth that would slowly become established, invading the whole world. Without Galileo the earth would still have revolved around the sun, but nobody knew that it moved. Religion and civilization at the time were universally founded on the false truth that the earth was a fixed point; and this worldwide belief sufficed to fix the point. "The earth revolves" turned everything upside down. The Church reeled and tottered on its foundation. The foundation had to be changed; everything had to be re-established on this henceforth revolving disk. There was a time, however, when people believed that the whole structure would collapse.

*I.*—So it is with other certainties that once seemed indispensable. We lose them and think the world is coming to an end. I am filled with wonder at the vast number of things the human body and mind can do without.

*HE.*—Doesn't it strike you as being an immense subject?

*I.*—Limitless would be a better word; and that is just

the reason why you had better be on your guard. The limitless is the paradise of idle visionaries.

At this last phrase he stiffened.

*HE.*—With all due respect, I believe that you understand very little of what I am saying. You seem to take me for an incorrigible romantic, of the type that used to proclaim:

> *Je ne puis. Malgré moi l'infini me tourmente*

—"Against my will, the infinite torments me." Well, I fully realize that such a mood produces nothing of value in art or life. . . . But already I feel sorry for having spoken frankly.

*I.*—You have nothing to regret; for I listened with care and understood you better than you seem to think. Might I venture to ask if your book is well under way?

*HE.*—Nothing has yet been written down, but it is all ripe in my head.

*I.*—When the fruit is ripe, it should be plucked. What you said was very interesting; I should like to hear more about it. . . . But now it is time for you to go. Don't come back until February. It will take me at least a fortnight to finish the introduction to the one-volume edition of Goethe's dramatic works that I promised to write for the Pléiade; the rest of the book is ready for the printer. I trust that your readers will consent to having Goethe occupy the space that would otherwise be devoted to our weekly interviews. Later we can go back to them.

And speaking of the limitless: did you know that it was Goethe's real drama?—that his constant and secret struggle was against the infinite, toward which he was driven by his too vast and universal genius, though all the time he felt and knew that any work of art, including his own life, necessarily involved limits and concentration, which were not to be achieved without many sacrifices.

One last remark: I wish you would stop believing in gulfs between us. If you (by which I mean your generation) go farther than we were able to go, why, so much the better! But remember that you must travel the same road, and that my hopes and best wishes will travel after, if indeed they haven't gone before you.

*An Introduction to*

# GOETHE'S DRAMATIC WORKS

CRITICISM has soon finished its task with certain authors, however great they may be. When a Mistral, for example, has received the tribute of a Maurras, the subject is exhausted, so to speak, and I find it hard to imagine that new fashions of praising him will be invented tomorrow. There are other authors, but they are rare, who offer a multiplicity of aspects for admiration, devotion, even hatred, and in whose realm the mind hesitates or delights to wander, as in some enchanted forest of Broceliande. It seems that they have never said their last word and that criticism has never discharged its debt to them. But more than this: it seems that their works and personalities are enlarged and enriched by the commentaries they call forth, the interpretations that distort them, and the insults they have to endure. Each commentary adds to the undergrowth that burgeons and blossoms around them. Deep in a thicket, the work itself almost disappears, and—particularly in Goethe's case—people declare themselves for or against, put forward their

opinions on the author of *Faust*, without ever having
examined the texts themselves, knowing them only by the
reactions they provoke in others. Ethical systems confront each other; camps are formed; Goethe ceases to
be primarily an author and becomes either a battlefield
or a rallying ground. But of what forces and what cre-
dos? These are the questions I shall try to answer. The
work of this man is so great in extent and importance;
his genius has manifested itself in so many diverse fashions, that the task is not at all simple; and I fear that
instead of defining a precise direction, I shall end merely
by expressing a tendency, an orientation of the mind.

# 1

The continual search for *lessons* in a work of art is
something that ordinarily gives me no pleasure, but
Goethe's works from first to last are instruction. His
genius seems essentially didactic. The desire, the need
to educate others by transmitting to them all the wisdom
he had been able to acquire during his lifetime remained
his dominant characteristic. We find evidence that this
desire was awakened in his earliest youth. Among the
stories told by Goethe's mother to Bettina von Arnim,
some of which are doubtless not to be accepted without
reservations, there is one so characteristic that it is hard
to question. Bettina tells us that little Wolfgang displayed so little sorrow over the death of a younger
brother, his constant playmate, that his mother scolded
him severely for what she regarded as his heartlessness.
"Tell me," she said, "had you no feeling at all for your

brother?" Full of outraged virtue, little Wolfgang ran to his room, crawled under the bed, and emerged with a thick bundle of papers covered with lessons and fables. "Here!" he exclaimed. "See all the things I wrote for his education."

This pedagogue in pinafores keeps reappearing in Goethe's youth. However justified was the reputation for egoism that would cling to him persistently, we can see that Goethe even then was always occupied with others, to such a degree that his egoism became, so to speak, all-embracing.

Everything in his life was instruction, edification, a means to culture; everything conspired toward a more perfect affirmation of himself and of all creatures. Every impulse of his will or intellect left eloquent traces that enable us not only to follow him wherever he went, but also to recognize in his work the reflection of his experience and the meditative echo of his loves, his strivings, his perplexities and embarrassments. When he tells us that he has written nothing but "occasional poems," we should understand that every occasion in his life became the stuff of poetry, and that his genius was largely ingenuity in directing his perpetual experiments toward representational and symbolic ends. There is nothing abstract or pedantic in his teaching. He could always say: "I was there. This is what befell me"; and besides feeling his continual presence, we shall believe that we were there ourselves. Nothing "befell" without his adding the inevitable: "By this is signified"—*et nunc erudimini.*

With Goethe the "I" quickly acquires a broader mean-

ing. Generalities are revealed in the individual, or, if you
will, the individual affirms himself as the symbol of a universal truth, its essence made manifest. Even in his most
relaxed and spontaneous moments Goethe is never dis-
tracted from himself; he continues to represent man's
striving toward culture. He does not abandon his efforts
toward an always more luminous perfection except to
plunge deeper into his subject and participate in the
harmony of an ordered universe. As soon as he ceases to
oppose, he collaborates. Whereas Hugo indulges his
verbal delirium by losing himself in orphic confusion,
Goethe, even in his most lyrical outpourings, tends to
guide us back toward the practical. His precepts,
aphorisms, apothegms are always—and this is their distinguishing mark—of good service. After the first unmo-
tivated lyricism of the tumultuous *Sturm und Drang*
period, we can find them everywhere in his work. Maxim
follows maxim at such short intervals that you think of
a smoker lighting one cigarette from another. There are
gracious, smiling, profound, and even inscrutable
maxims; but I am afraid that there are others which, in
translation and deprived of their luster, will appear almost silly.

To arouse the emotion of the reader or spectator seems
to him only incidental, since he is aiming beyond and
through this emotion at another goal, that of a supreme
edification. Goethe wishes neither to surprise nor to over-
awe us, but rather to persuade us gently; to instill in us
the feeling, not of a moral obligation or a duty, but
rather of a knowledge and a power; to make us better ac-
quainted with the great laws and thereby to raise us

above them. Then, from this elevation, we can learn how to render the great laws useful and employ them for human ends.

There is no absorption of himself in others, such as one finds with Shakespeare. There is no frenzied love for others, in the Christian manner of Dostoyevsky. Goethe feels and wishes himself to be representative; let us say with more exactness, to be exemplary. He seems to have entered the world for that sole purpose: "to serve as an example to the universe." "*Wie ich euch ein Beispiel gebe*" —let me be your example: these are the last words he gives to Egmont. And having accepted this role, Goethe assumes it completely, conscientiously, and with a self-confidence that soon becomes faith in a sort of fatality. He is among the elect; he is in tune with destiny, with God. A demon, *his* demon, guides him and urges him forward; if he obeys the demon, he can walk through fire unscathed; hence he is willing to follow him into evil paths. For he feels that happiness is not the object of his search; or at least he would regard it as happiness to achieve his destiny; nothing else matters. Thus we shall see his Egmont, supported to the end by the friendship of young Ferdinand, the Duke of Alba's son, regain his joy in life a moment before being marched to the headsman's block; and we shall hear him cry: "I cease to live, but I have lived; my friend, live in the same fashion, gladly and passionately; and fear not death." [1]

---

[1] *Ich höre auf zu leben, aber ich habe gelebt; so leb' auch du, mein Freund, gern und mit Lust, und scheue den Tod nicht.*—*Egmont*, Act V. The line from *Andromaque* that follows is *Hé bien, je meurs content et mon sort est rempli.* Gide misquoted it, writing *rôle* for *sort*—but see the following interview.—Tr.

"So be it! I die content and my destiny is fulfilled,"
said Racine's Orestes; and there is more in his speech
than the insanely bitter irony that appears on the surface. Racine, fully conscious of this tragic grandeur,
permits Orestes to taste for a moment, before going mad
with grief, the supreme joy of a hero: to assume his
*exemplary* role. "I was born to serve as an example";
and he feels that he is now the accomplished model of evil
fortune, "*du malheur un modèle accompli.*"

There can be no question, for Goethe, of duties arbi-
trarily imposed or of a society in which all men are
equalized under a common uniform; and no more can
there be a question of submitting any work of art to pre-
established rules that are independent of itself. Every
human being is born to bear witness—*et testis esto*—and
shirks his duty if he does not fully assume this mission
of manifesting as best he can his individual truth. There
is no categorical imperative. To each his own fate.

Let us acknowledge, moreover, that Goethe's fate was
far from being disagreeable; the lines fell to him in pleas-
ant places. It must also be said that, since he set great
store by equilibrium and serenity, he refused to be deeply
troubled by any passion or rendered headstrong by any
conviction. . . . But I shall come back later to what I
should consent to call his *opportunism* only after ex-
plaining that the word is not being used in any depre-
ciatory sense.

Doubtless it is much too late to protest against the
false picture of Goethe that prevailed for a long time in
France, where he was once regarded as a sort of Olym-
pian divinity, impassive, insensitive and unperturbed.

That Goethe could love, suffer, and even feel compassion is no longer questioned; today there are very few critics who seek to magnify his intellect at the expense of his humanity. But this much remains: every feeling that attached him to common mortals resulted in some work of art. Everything served him; which is to say that he made use of everything and that there was no adversity from which, in the last resort, he failed to profit. He had the gift of finding a lesson in every experience in which he did not find pleasure; but pleasure taught him its lessons too. Not only his passions but his sufferings were productive. "Poetry is liberation," he said. What does he mean by this maxim, if not that the intense cultivation of his emotions, his love affairs, his sorrows even, and their transmutation into poems, set him free?

There is nothing more natural than to liberate oneself, or at least try to be liberated, from something painful. The extraordinary, the admirable trait in Goethe is that he also liberates himself from happiness, from a love that has given him nothing but joy. Satisfaction in his case implies a *satis:* it is enough. That was the secret of his power: to liberate himself as soon as he was satisfied. After having made use of happiness, after directing it toward poetic ends, after drawing from it everything suitable to art, Goethe did not linger, but went on; he kept love in his heart only so long as he needed it for his work. Hence each of Goethe's love poems is a little like a monument or a commemorative trophy: *in memoriam.*

Let others grow indignant at what they will describe as conceit or self-centeredness. To me it seems not so much pride as a fashion of paying one's debt to the world and of permitting oneself to keep nothing intimate or personal. As soon as anything particular happens to Goethe, he transforms it immediately into a generality. He feels and wishes himself, I repeat, to be *exemplary.* He exists only in order to tell us what he is. Judging him from this point of view (and I think it offers the best approach), could one find a "representative of humanity" who was more moral than Goethe?—more conscious of himself and always faithful to his duty?—or one who was more constantly disciplined in a more intelligent fashion? He is the man who, among all others, carries out his mission.

In his *Philosophical Dialogues* Renan makes Theoctistes say: "The divine effort that resides in all is brought forth by just men, by savants, by artists. Each has his part. Goethe's duty was to be selfish for his work. The transcendent immorality of the artist becomes in its fashion a supreme morality, if it leads to the accomplishment of the particular but divine mission with which each of us is charged here below." I had already written the preceding paragraphs when I chanced upon these lines, which admirably summarize my conclusions.

It is no concern of ours that the impertinent Dumas *fils* could see nothing in Goethe but a "venerable goat." He made the remark soon after 1870, when he was full of anti-Germanic ire. Those were the days when French writers were also being taken to task. In 1872 one magazine circulated a questionnaire dealing with "literary *corruption* in France," and many of the answers denounced the pernicious influence of Goethe on the French

—as if all other nations had escaped his evil qualities!
It is easy to see at a distance that such accusations were
absurd. In those days, however, we lived in the shadow
of defeat and were trying to regain our self-respect. On
the ground that the social reorganization and moral reform of our country were the most urgent tasks, we insisted on closing our ears to every voice from beyond
the Rhine. Moreover, what could we learn from an author
who, it was said, professed an irreverent lack of concern
for religion and patriotism? In the midst of the French
effort toward national salvation, Goethe *en prit pour
son grade*, as the soldiers say; he was given the repri-
mand that suited his rank.

## 2

I do not see in Goethe the surprising originality that
sets its seal on acts and works. From early manhood he
displayed a constant desire to understand the laws that
govern the world of nature and the world of men, but
also to use those laws to the best advantage, rather than
setting against them an inviolable personality. It was
from the universal laws of nature that Goethe derived
his notion of the only God whom he recognized, revered,
and served. As for the common and variable laws of men,
one could obey them with an easy smile while turning
them to good use; they govern society and change as it
changes; but society needs them for its survival (and
without society there would be no culture). He says to
us: "Creatures dependent on the moment, on the chang-

ing weather, on good and evil fortune! Will you never
learn to endure them both with equanimity? [2]

Goethe did not long remain a rebel. A moment ago I
spoke of his "opportunism." What I meant was that he
proposed to turn all circumstances, fortunate and un-
fortunate, to the best possible advantage, both for himself (but not in the hope of any material profit) and
for his work. His aim was to choose, from the circumstances of his life, everything that was least episodic,
most common and—since it was recognized by all—most
capable of being made useful to all. He was able to fix
these elements in the best and most appropriate form.

The re-establishment of human dignity, which is the
goal that Goethe proposes to each man, is not achieved
solely or principally by revolt, but rather by patiently
considering divine and human laws, and by learning to
use all the virtues, to direct all the energies of our nature.
It is not to be obtained without limitations on ourselves
—that is to say, without sacrifice. If Goethe's first word
of wisdom is *Entwicklung*, development, the second will
be *Entsagung*, renunciation, which no doubt is less pleas-
ant to the ear and more difficult to understand, but which
nevertheless remains the indispensable helpmate of the
other.

Yes, Goethe was quick to admit that every development, beginning with his own, implies a choice and that

[2] *Vom Augenblick abhängig, Spiel der Witterung,*
  *Des Glücks und Unglücks! Keins von beiden wiszt ihr je*
  *Zu bestehn mit Gleichmut.*
                                        *Faust II*, Act III

every choice implies a sacrifice; a plant cannot give sap at the same moment to all its buds. This voluntary limitation of his multiple latent faculties remained the secret drama of his life. That every gesture is a promise; that each depends on all else and all others; that no man can regard himself as a "lone horseman": these are the principles he persuaded himself to accept, and they keep his counsel from being purely selfish, as it was formerly thought to be; it is also a counsel of obedience. Its eloquence comes from the fact that Goethe himself had once been in revolt (and the Romantics of his younger days halted at this first stage of his teaching). Nothing could be more rebellious than the monologue from his *Prometheus*, which was printed by itself in his early collections of verse: the Titan defies Zeus and proclaims his contempt for the brute forces by which he was overpowered, thundering against them with all the impious strength of his insubordination. Now, if each of Goethe's works is instructive when taken alone, we can learn even more from the succession of his works; that is, from the quite logical order in which they appeared. This extravagant monologue takes place in a drama, and soon it is merely a moment in the drama. Goethe had to learn manners, customs, and the art of directing men. His important functions at the court of the Grand Duke, his post as director of the Weimar theater, his responsibilities as a lover—everything warned him against the disorder that follows inevitably from the exercise of too great liberties. Having demanded sacrifices from himself as a matter of duty, he wished also to obtain them from others. Hence the counsels of temperance that abound more and more in Goethe's work as he grows older; for, when they lacked such wisdom, "Countless minds have been ruined by their own force and suppleness," as Montaigne told us in his day.

In his dramatic works the extraordinary equilibrium of his faculties permits him to inhabit each in turn Faust and Mephistopheles, Iphigenia and Thoas, Tasso and Antonio, even—or very nearly—the implacable Duke of Alba and the free, the too free Egmont: on the one side, the embodiments of everything most generous in the human spirit; on the other side, the representatives of chastening order. The defeat he portrays in *Werther* (but this is a work of early manhood) might easily have been his own. Goethe, however, would not consent to be vanquished; he was also able, and without great effort, to become that which triumphed over Werther. Order, laws, decorum, established society, discipline of the fiery instincts: all these find something in him that understands and approves. But since he equally understands all the rest—both passion and that which rightfully holds passion in check, but without stifling it; both revolt and its pacification; both the cause of the individual and that of the State—it is the conflict between these rival forces that will nourish his work, and principally his plays; with the increasing serenity that is the triumph of order. But we note that this order has injured nothing and suppressed nothing; that it takes everything into account and gives everyone his rightful share, to the extent that no one else is harmed; that it puts everything in its proper place.

Unfortunately a first draft of *Torquato Tasso*, dating

from 1780, has not been preserved. Everything leads us
to suppose that Tasso's tragedy began by being much
like Werther's and that Goethe's aim in the beginning
was to depict an unhappy love, with the subjective ideal-
ism of his hero straining to break the chains of conven-
tion and clashing with the reasonable and pragmatic
hostility of a rival. But, as Gundolf quite rightly says,
"When the *Tasso* was finished, in 1789, the external
enemy had become the incarnation of an internal principle, a symbol of the just moral barriers against which
Tasso's exasperated subjectivity was shattered." As a
result of Goethe's personal experiences during those
nine years, at the court of Weimar and in his official
posts, the figure of Antonio had grown larger and more
solid—"so much so that, in the drama, it balances the
poetic hero and becomes his rightful competitor."

The very long first scene of the second act (the dialogue between Tasso and the Princess Leonora d'Este,
sister of Alphonso II, the Duke of Ferrara) is based
wholly on this debate. Tasso regrets the radiance of the
golden age that acknowledged only a single rule of conduct: everything that pleases (*Was gefällt*) is permissible. "That age may come again," the Princess tells
him, "but we must change one word in the adage: everything proper (*Was sich ziemt*) is permissible." A discussion begins, a tournament of ideas and not a mere parade:
the defense of "what is proper," of decorum, is the prov-
ince of high-minded women. "Man aspires to freedom;
woman to propriety."

By what miracle of art without artifice does this dialogue maintain its interest from beginning to end, never

ceasing to be rich in emotion and quivering with life?
There is an admirable moderation in everything the
Princess has to say, although it is almost a declaration
of love; she never ceases to be mistress of her heart. In
this respect she is quite different from Racine's heroines,
who make involuntary confessions (there is almost always something *malgré soi* in Racine), whereas Leonora
d'Este's half-confession is conscious, voluntary, measured, and her decorum is the better part of her grace. And
when Tasso, the poet, lets himself be carried away, she
interrupts his lyrical flight:

> No further, Tasso! Many things there are
> That we may hope to win with violence;
> While others only can become our own
> Through moderation and wise self-restraint.
> Such, it is said, is virtue, such is love,
> Which is allied to her. Think well on this.[3]

Goethe will not rest until he has found and given to
each of his characters the exact phrase, the maxim in
which a whole moral code is concentrated. Two examples
will cast light on what I am trying to say. There is
nothing more exceptional and bizarre to the point of
being absurd than little Homunculus in his crystal
prison; in the flask where Wagner, Faust's disciple, has

---

3 This is the Anna Swanwick translation (1850), which is old-
fashioned but fairly accurate. In the original:

> *Nicht weiter, Tasso! Viele Dinge sind's*
> *Die wir mit Heftigkeit ergreifen sollen:*
> *Doch andre können nur durch Massigung*
> *Und durch Entbehren unser eigen werden.*
> *So sagt man, sei die Tugend, sei die Liebe,*
> *Die ihr verwandt ist. Das bedenke wohl!*

just created him. Only the tiny image of a man, he still has life, he still is able to express himself. And what he says is a maxim of such general application that one begins to suspect Goethe of having seized upon this truth long before and of having imagined Homunculus merely in order to express it. *"Was künstlich ist verlangt geschlossnen Raum."* All art requires a closed space: it is an aphorism that soon became famous.

My second example is also taken from *Faust II.* In quoting the versicles charged with emotion and meaning that Goethe puts into the mouths of the diligent tribe of Dactyls, I feel all the more pleasure because these remarkable lines, to the best of my knowledge, have rarely been cited:

> Who will free us?
> We smelt the iron
> From which they forge our chains.
> O deliverance
> Do not tarry!
> While we are waiting
> Let us be pliant.[4]

---

[4] This is a literal translation from Gide, not from Goethe. Comparing it with the original (printed below) we find that Gide made little changes of his own, so that the stanza would apply to the French as well as to the diligent tribe of Dactyls.—Tr.

> *Wer wird uns retten!*
> *Wir schaffen 's Eisen,*
> *Sie schmieden Ketten.*
> *Uns loszureiszen*
> *Ist noch nicht zeitig;*
> *Drum seid geschmeidig!*

No translation, alas, can render the mordant quality
of these little verses, with their strong rhythm and feminine rhymes, any more than it can render the harmonious
unfolding of the unrhymed iambic pentameters of *Torquato Tasso* and *Iphigenia in Tauris*. We hear them
without tiring, as we might watch the waves sinking to
rest on a beach when the storm has died away.

What I have said until now scarcely explains how
Goethe's influence, which seems so reasonable, came to be
regarded as pernicious. In whose eyes? Oh, principally
and almost solely in those of Catholic writers. Barbey
d'Aurevilly, Ernest Hello, Léon Bloy, and Paul Claudel
are among those who belabored him with insults based on
a resolute lack of understanding and who tried to push
him aside contemptuously. Other Christians, more per-
spicacious, were quick to recognize Goethe as their most
dangerous adversary.

The superlative is justified by the importance of this
life and these works, by their extraordinary success, by
their capacity to influence others, by their splendor. Yet
Goethe did not attack Christianity, as Voltaire and
Diderot had done before him and Nietzsche would do; he
simply passed over it; or rather he passed to one side.
Original sin, repentance, and redemption were no concern of his. Moreover, he must have felt that the evocation of Christ on the cross was intolerable; he turned his
head away, as he did from all painful spectacles. Accus-
tomed to it as we are from childhood, we have ceased to
feel the horror of this image, regarding it much more as

a symbol than as the depiction of a real and revolting torture. It is the sign, for each Christian, not of a martyrdom but of his own redemption.

To all these ideas Goethe remained deaf. It is true that he adopted a "Christian mythology" for the medieval needs of his *Faust*, but without any deeper conviction than he adopted Persian mythology for his *East-Westerly Divan*. ("When he uses Catholic rituals for artistic purposes, Goethe is, of course, *allegorical* at the end of the second *Faust;* he had recourse to the symbols of a religion whose principles did not agree with his own, unlike those of the Greeks," we read in Volume II of Gundolf.) Nevertheless he remained extremely sensitive to the piety of others, being pious himself in his fashion and, as he said, having a spirit "naturally prone to veneration."

Catholicism finds it easier to struggle against impiety than against a different piety; and everything would be well, episcopally speaking, if Goethe had been content to threaten the Christian hold on our souls with nothing but indiscipline and abandonment to one's whims. We have seen, however, that what he proposed to others and to himself was something quite different from mere license. To begin with, he did not regard man as a fallen creature, but as one who depended only on himself and had no need of a Saviour. Catholicism anticipates our anguish, our weakness; it is there to comfort us. Goethe tries to make us serene; he maintains himself in that state and, dying, he is reabsorbed in God as in a supreme harmony.

If we sought for implorations and cries for help in Goethe's work, we should seek in vain; the only prayers he permits himself are those of thanksgiving. The only God recognized by Goethe is confused with Nature and with the Whole of which the poet himself is a part. And it is as part of the divine Whole that Goethe respects and honors himself. His individuality is comprised in his adoration, and his duties toward himself derive from his duties toward God. If he does not feel the need of God, it is because he seeks and finds Him everywhere in the cosmos, although not by closing his eyes to the outer world. He no more acknowledges a personal God than he believes in miracles and revelations. He has never felt the avid thirst of the mystics. What makes him hostile to Christianity is the suprasensible satisfaction it proposes to the soul, its turning aside from physical researches ("Christ: eternal thief of energies," Rimbaud would later say), its depreciation of what he holds to be real for the sake of the imaginary; it is the contempt for the body, for matter; it is sanctity.

His journey to Italy has been put forward as the determining cause of his paganism. I should rather say that this contact with ancient Rome and Hellenism merely revealed his paganism to himself. He is as naturally and spontaneously pagan as Pater's Marius and Corneille's Pauline have essentially Christian souls. But Goethe's paganism does not stop short with the Olympians. It is through adoration of a power superior to Zeus himself that his Prometheus is driven to revolt, Zeus signifying for Goethe those elemental forces that the spirit must contrive to master.

## 3

Yes, Goethe triumphed over himself and the world, but one begins to wonder whether his triumphs weren't sometimes a little easy (even though the idea of merit is out of place in this discussion). Then one remembers what Nietzsche wrote about other victories, that they might sometimes cheapen or *de-moralize* the victor; and one is forced to admit that Goethe's demon, surrounded by the fruits of his success, was becoming somewhat middle-class. Heaped with honors all during his life, with triumphs of every sort; a man of property, courted and coddled, he had even the good fortune to meet, toward the close of his life, a zealous Eckermann who was devoted without being obsequious and who had just enough servility to furnish a stepladder to his glory, so that access to the genius was simple and the genius, stepping down a little, could more easily receive his due homage. . . . He attained a very advanced age without losing his faculties; he died without agony, surfeited with everything. . . . How then does he dare to speak of "renunciation"? Renunciation of what? Doubtless of a certain instinctive fervor that was revealed in the ebullience of his youth. Goethe, the rebel of yesterday, grew temperate and decorous—ah, blessed virtue! He renounced. And soon we see him retreating almost to the other side of the world from that high promontory, that rock on which he had once been exposed by his genius. Somewhere concealed in the word "renunciation" is there not a longing for the driven spray?—some secret regret for everything that was generous or heroic in the wildness of his youth?

Having paid Goethe our tribute, let us continue with our summing up for the prosecution.

We are a little embarrassed, or at least perplexed, by his attitude toward Napoleon, as well as by the opportunism I mentioned before; in this case it caused him to display the Legion of Honor on his breast, to the horror of his more patriotic fellow citizens, at a time when it would have seemed more fitting not to boast of his decoration and not to derive material advantages from something that wounded his country. But Goethe was still dazzled (as how could he fail to be?) by a dream that seemed on the point of being realized: the dream of a pacific and glorious unification of all Europe, one that might have cost most of the smaller states their autonomy and their reason for being, but that would have given at least to Weimar and at least to himself, Goethe, an even greater importance, while preserving all his liberty of thought. Moreover, how could he fail to be flattered (and Goethe was extremely, almost childishly susceptible to praise) by the particular consideration he received? "You are a man, Monsieur Goethe," the Emperor said.

"In that case, you are another, Sire, as I am glad to acknowledge."

I can imagine him thinking these words, almost speaking them. And nothing leads us to suppose that he would perhaps have been disillusioned by what followed; for Napoleon had a sense of and a respect for values. This, indeed, was precisely what Goethe could glimpse in the future: that he would be taken and used at his full value.

The truth is that he felt himself to be little affected by historical events; in the proper sense of the word, they did not interest him. His influence had spread far beyond the borders of the little Grand Duchy of Weimar and beyond all Germany; now that Napoleon was creating a unified Europe by force of arms, Goethe would lord over it by spiritual force; he would broaden his fatherland to include a continent. His mind was at rest as soon as he knew that he would retain his freedom of thought, and that the invasion would not upset his little collections of natural-history specimens, of ancient art in plaster casts, of engravings and medallions: all this was his life, his real life. Not once was Goethe touched by the shadow of fear that the very soil from which he sprang and on which his genius rested might tremble and disappear beneath him. In short, nothing close to his heart was threatened, and he might well anticipate, quite on the contrary, that . . . Enough of this; let us respect his tranquillity.

Goethe the naturalist was not in the least a historian. On this point he left no doubt, saying that history concerned him only as a subject matter for his poems. He occupied himself with the permanent, not with the episodic; with what recurred necessarily, in obedience to eternal laws, not with anything produced by accidental circumstances and never repeated. One remembers his conversation with Eckermann soon after the French revolution of 1830, which had caused no little excitement in Germany. "Well!" Goethe cried, hastening toward him. "What do you think of the news? The volcano is in eruption; everything is taking fire; this will be the end of little discussions behind locked doors."

"A frightful story," Eckermann answered, "but it was no more than you could expect with such a ministry. Considering all the circumstances, the royal family . . ."

Goethe interrupted him: "We are talking at cross-purposes, my dear friend; I wasn't speaking about those people at all. My concern was with something quite different. I was referring to the statement that Geoffroy de Saint-Hilaire has just made before the Academy of Sciences; his dispute with Cuvier is of the greatest importance. . . ."

I therefore like to imagine the extreme interest that Goethe would have shown in the recent advances of science; doubtless not so much in practical inventions, like the airplane, the telephone, the motion-picture camera, as in the discoveries capable of transforming our picture of the cosmos—that of Einstein, which sets our best-established notions of physics and geometry tottering on their foundations; that of radium, leading us to question the permanence of matter; and those others that were made precisely in the realms to which Goethe would pay no attention, thinking as he did that mortal scientists could never reach them or at least could find nothing profitable there: astronomy, paleontology, the origins of the solar system, of our earth, of matter, of life. Why trouble one's head with such questions? "The life of man," he said to Eckermann (October 3, 1828), "is sufficiently overburdened with his passions and misfortunes, generally speaking, without his feeling the additional need of plunging into the shadows of a barbarous past. What he needs is clarity and cheering influences. (*Er bedarf der Klarheit und der Aufheiterung.*)" A few days later (October 7), stimulated by a general conversation and urged to give his opinions on the creation of man, Goethe returned to the same theme: "As for racking one's brains to learn how the thing happened, I regard that as an idle occupation, one we should leave to those who pass their time with insoluble problems because they have nothing better to do." This is a remark that he would doubtless not dare to make today, after researches into these "insoluble problems" have led to unhoped-for results and have put scientists on the road to some of their most fruitful discoveries.

It is the custom to rhapsodize over his thirst for clarity; everybody admires his last words: "*Mehr Licht!*" although nobody knows whether to interpret them as a simple demand for more light or a cry of thankful recognition at a celestial vision. (Believers are skilled in giving a mystical interpretation to the last stammered words of the dying.) On the contrary, I should choose to deplore this horror of obscurity, which I hold to be Goethe's most serious weakness and error. It is the point at which he approaches Voltaire, the point at which Shakespeare and Dante draw away from him, not fearing for their part to plunge ahead, one among mournful shades, the other into the black gulfs of the human soul. Goethe, on his side, prefers to live in sunlight; he has no eyes except for the luminous colors of the prism; and doubtless nothing would have astonished him more than to learn (but in his days who would have suspected?) that the rainbow concealed anything whatever in its dark

fringes. And yet he realized that the Mothers—those
mysterious matrices of everything that has form and
life—waited and watched in the shadows beyond the day.
Why did he fail to overcome his horror of darkness and
fail to put more questions to the "Mouth of Shadow" in
the effort to seize upon some of its secrets?

And now we ask ourselves: however great, noble,
and serenely beautiful was the human image that Goethe
left behind him, does it wholly satisfy us? He was the
reasoning man, logical and cultured to the highest degree; but piercing through all this wisdom I hear the
voice of St. Paul: "Would to God ye could bear with me
a little in my folly." [5] I also remember Schiller and his
lesson of heroism; and I say to myself that there was
nothing more admirable in Goethe's life than the friendship between these two. Standing before his death mask,
with its eyelids forever closed on so much inner serenity,
I evoke the ravaged or tragic masks of Dante, of Pascal,
of Beethoven, of Nietzsche, of Leopardi; their voices had
deeper tones. Hölderlin, before sinking into madness, had
also turned his eyes toward the radiance of Greece; and
today his poetry affects us even more than Goethe's
*Roman Elegies*, for all their splendor. Finally, after
Goethe has gorged himself with all the good things of
this earth while talking about "renunciation," does he
wish us to believe that his arms could have held more
than he embraced?—that he might have taken still more?
Or, speaking more seriously, might the question not be:
Did Goethe embrace the best? And what is the best for

[5] II Corinthians xi, 1.

man, the highest good to which nothing else is to be preferred?

Christians alone have the right to ask this first and supreme question. That it never disturbed Goethe's serenity is precisely what concerns us here. And Goethe would cease to be Goethe if doubt or suffering had added the pathetic touch of a few wrinkles to the patiently acquired calm of this admirable effigy. We remain grateful to Goethe, for he gives us the finest example, both smiling and solemn, of what man can obtain by and from himself, without recourse to Grace.

# IMAGINARY INTERVIEW · 11[1]

HE HAD, so he told me, some remarks to offer on the subject of the "Introduction to Goethe's Dramatic Works" that had kept us apart for a whole month; but first he wanted to know whether I was satisfied with what I had done.

"No!" I exclaimed. "There was a mistake in the line I quoted from Racine. This is the second time it has happened and I cannot forgive myself. No doubt the error would have struck me at once, as it did later when I reread my introduction in *Le Figaro;* but I didn't see proofs, a fact that is hardly enough to excuse me. I have often complained about inaccurate quotations, but they irritate me less in the case of others than when I make them myself."

*HE.*—If you please, let us drop this subject that chiefly concerns your injured self-esteem. I wanted to bring up a much more serious criticism.

*I (interrupting him).*—And while I happen to think

---

1 This interview did not appear in the French text of *Interviews Imaginaires,* the manuscript having been lost in transit.—Tr.

of it . . . the little picture I mentioned at our last meeting, as you probably remember; the seascape that I said was a Derain; it is a Braque. I was thinking of the right name when I used the other, and I still can't understand how I happened to go wrong.

*HE.*—I was surprised too. But what I have to say impresses me as being more—

*I.*—And still another error: a correspondent mentions a line from *Faust*, to which he says, and quite justly, that I gave the wrong interpretation. It was the little aphorism of Homunculus:

*Was künstlich ist verlangt geschlossnen Raum.*

*HE.*—Which you translated, if I remember correctly: "All art requires a closed space."

*I.*—My correspondent objects that the word *künstlich* does not apply to art, but to artifice. If it had been a question of art, Goethe would have said *künstlerisch*. The lesson implied by the verse is therefore quite different: as an artificial creature, Homunculus cannot live except in his bottle, where a crystal wall protects him; in the open air he would dissolve.

*HE.*—Yes, I see. It is a point over which we might quibble for hours. But I wanted to draw your attention to—

*I.*—And that reminds me of a remark made long ago by Odilon Redon. You have almost forgotten him today, since your eyes are dazzled by the still bolder experiments of other painters. But in my early days, when we disciples of Mallarmé were engaged in a violent revolt against realism, we looked toward Redon as a master;

or more than that, as a magician skilled in peopling canvas or paper with a mass of incomplete organisms, haggard protozoans and homunculi suspended in a dream, as one might see them through the glass walls of an aquarium, floating in a fluid felicity. We pored over his lithographs as over Mallarmé's latest sonnets, in an aura of mystical adoration. But to come to the point, a young artist visited Redon to ask his advice, and the master repeated (in a mild voice, for he was the most benevolent of creatures) this guiding maxim that summed up his whole æsthetic theory: "Close yourself up with nature."

*HE.*—As a result of its struggles against naturalism or realism, we now recognize, dear master, that art, or at least the literary art, in the days when you wrote your *Nourritures terrestres,* "had somewhat the smell of a closed room," as I think you said at the time. But, with the privilege of returning later, let us pass on to another subject. As I said before, I wanted to make what seems to me a grave criticism of your "Introduction." You give your readers the impression (and I am thinking particularly of certain phrases at the end of the essay) ; you make us feel, I repeat, that each man is obliged to choose between the Christian position and the one adopted by Goethe. But the truth is that there are many avenues of escape from the moral dominance of Christianity without following Goethe's path.

*I.*—And yet the examples I cited, those of Nietzsche, Leopardi, Hölderlin (and I might have mentioned many others), should leave no doubt of what I meant to say. Goethe does not teach heroism, and we have need of heroes. Christianity can lead us to heroism, of which one of the highest forms is sanctity; but every hero is not necessarily a Christian. Free thought does not always wear the indulgent smile of Renan, the sarcastic smile of Voltaire or the flippant smile of Anatole France. Men have gone to their death as martyrs although they had no dogmas to guide them and were supported only by their simple probity of spirit. It was a martyrdom without glory or hope of future recompense, and for that reason it was all the more admirable. Without following in their footsteps, let us say that human dignity, and the sort of moral carriage or *consistency* on which our hopes now depend, are capable of dispensing with the support and comfort of Faith.

*HE.*—Perhaps. There are scattered cases. But don't you think that only a common faith can unite the energies that have certainly not ceased to exist in France, although you yourself have often complained of their disorientation? From your past writings, I could easily assemble statements to the effect that discipline, and even a sort of enlistment, are not necessarily opposed to a certain individualism—"individualism rightly understood," as you formerly said.

*I.*—Yes; I was speaking of communism, and since then I have had to change my tune. The Christian religion undoubtedly shows more respect for the human personality than does communism.

*HE.*—Which shows no respect for it whatever, as you must have recognized.

*I.*—I also recognize that our present task is to unite, to be united.

*HE.*—In the realm of the spirit, there are moments

and even historical periods of expansion or diastole, just as there are for the heart.

*I.*—And we are now in a period of systole; one might say in its very midst.

*HE.*—Let me remind you of the lines you quoted from Goethe, with a somewhat free translation:

> O deliverance
> Do not tarry!

*I.*—It was because I was trying to preserve their rhythm.

> *Uns loszureiszen*
> *Ist noch nicht zeitig*

simply means, as I realize, that the time of diastole is still to come.

*HE.*—What you presented as an impatient desire was merely a statement of fact.

*I.*—But the first line of the stanza: "Who will free us?" seemed to justify an impulse that came straight from my heart.

*HE.*—In these days we must learn to repress many of our impulses.

*I.*—I have just found a line or two from Tacitus that calmed my heart again, for the moment: "*Memoriam quoque ipsam cum voce perdidessemus, si tam in nostra potestate esset oblivisci quam tacere.*"

*HE.*—Do you read Latin easily?

*I.*—Not at all; but the sentence is exceptionally limpid. Usually I have to glance at a translation. Here is the one that André Cordier gives: "We should have lost memory itself along with speech, if it had been as much in our power to forget as to be silent." In that whole section of the *Life of Agricola* there are reflections I should like to discuss with you, when we are again in a period of diastole. In these days of systole we shall confine ourselves to literature. Might I ask if you have been working on your book since I last saw you?

*HE.*—To tell the truth, I haven't. But it is ripening. My greatest difficulty is that I should like to confine myself to what is essential, general, and universal.

*I.*—My dear friend, always bear in mind that works of art have no way of achieving the general except through and by means of the particular. That is what Goethe never forgot. Otherwise you must yield your place to the philosophers, for they are more at home with generalities.

# IMAGINARY INTERVIEW · 12

## *St. Mallarmé the Esoteric*

*HE.*—During our last conversation you happened to speak of sanctity, saying, if I remember correctly, that it was among the highest forms of heroism. Wouldn't it be better to confine the word to its strictly religious meaning?

*I.*—It is rather the meaning of the word "heroism" that I should like to restrict and qualify. When I say that we need heroes, I hope you will understand that I am not talking about novels this time. Heroism does not begin until a certain inertia has been overcome, or until a person demands more of himself than he can comfortably give. I am not trying to offer a definition of the word, for that can be found in a dictionary; rather I am using it to describe a particular order of virtues. It sometimes happens that heroes are created by external circumstances. During a battle, a fire, or a shipwreck, quite undistinguished people whose virtues had remained dormant may reveal a devotion that amazes themselves. The saint, on the other hand, does not wait for this provocation or command; he is possessed by a secret

*(110)*

need; he wishes to rise above the miserable condition of ordinary humankind by obtaining from himself more, still more, the best; he is not easily satisfied. Doubtless he is urged forward by religious zeal and continually admonished by the God to whom he listens in his heart. He is not surprised by himself nor filled with admiration at his deeds; no matter how lofty his flight, he still falls short of the perfection at which he aims; and always he suffers from a sense of his own unworthiness, his insufficiency.

*HE.*—Aren't you describing a quality that artists may also possess?

*I.*—A few exceptional artists, it is true; and we admire and venerate them for that reason by itself, almost independently of their work. Let us agree that every artist applies himself to his work as best he can. But many other preoccupations are involved that have nothing to do with art; he thinks of money, success, his public standing. No, the men who disregard their private interests and behave toward their ideal (I can find no other word) as saints behave toward the Master who told them: "My kingdom is not of this world"—such artists are very rare. I was thinking particularly of Flaubert and Mallarmé.

*HE.*—You say that in this respect your admiration for the man is independent of your admiration for his work?

*I.*—One moment: I admire the work of Mallarmé, the work of Flaubert; and on this fact depends my admiration for the lives of both men. But the strange dominion that Mallarmé exercised (oh, without claiming to do so) over certain members of my generation was something that owed no more to his work than it did to his conduct of life; to the unusual example of disinterestedness that he set before us.

*HE.*—Isn't that disinterestedness precisely the quality for which he is being condemned today? The young poets I know claim either to "think with their hands," as Denis de Rougemont says, or at least to regard poetry as a form of participation in life. They protest that the isolation of the poet, resulting from his adherence to the religion of art, was extremely harmful both to poetry, which began to wither when it lost contact with the masses, and to the masses as well, since they were weaned away from poetry.

*I.*—Every age has new problems to confront. It may be that the relationship between the spiritual and the temporal is one of the chief problems today. Nevertheless I pity the young poet who lets himself be obsessed with it.

*HE.*—Do you want the poet to be unconcerned with the matters that now preoccupy our thoughts and weigh upon our hearts? Do you want him to live as if on the margins of the world? Do you want him to keep out of difficulties by "making himself scarce," in every meaning of the phrase?

*I.*—No. There is part of his nature that can and should lend itself to the sad business of human transactions. "I pray not that thou shouldest take them out of the world, but that thou shouldest keep them from the evil," was what the apostle said.

*HE.*—St. Paul was not thinking of poets.

*I.*—No matter; for what he said applies to them

equally. It is not a good thing, for example; it may compromise both his work and the development of his ideas, if the poet depends on that work for his living. In order to think and write freely, Mallarmé, who was wholly possessed by his strange poetic apostleship, spent thirty years as a professor of English in secondary schools. Often the poet must have a double trade, a fact that recently prompted Duhamel to make some very wise observations. Those of us who lived in Mallarmé's circle were ashamed of the very idea that literature could be made to "pay." I remember the scandal that was caused in those days by Jean de Tinan, the author of *Do You Hope to Succeed?* Speaking to his colleagues on the editorial committee of the *Centaure,* he told us not to be suckers, *"des poires"*; he was through with all that foolishness and in the future he would not deliver his copy unless he was paid for it. The rest of us felt that writing for money was "selling ourselves" in the worst sense of the term. We were not to be purchased; and our thoughts turned to Mallarmé. In those days it seemed to us that Barrès, by entering politics, had forsworn himself and fallen from his glory.

*HE.*—In those days, too, Zola's novels were selling by the millions of copies.

*I.*—Mallarmé never had the slightest tone of contempt when he mentioned them; it was simply that he was seeking for something else, something that seemed to us of infinitely greater value.

*HE.*—After what you began by saying, this would give me to understand that you regarded Mallarmé as a saint.

*I.*—We most certainly felt admiration for his poetry; for himself, for the man, it was veneration. He was a believer, a zealot.

*HE.*—A dreamer with his head in the clouds; one who played at give-away and loser-take-all, in the manner of the mystics. It might have been said that he was dazzled by shadows.

*I.*—And that he preferred the shadow to the living prey. Hence these verses:

> *Ma faim qui d'aucuns fruits ici ne se régale*
> *Trouve en leur docte manque une saveur égale.*[1]

*HE.*—Do you approve of his depreciating the real to the greater glory of the imaginary?

*I.*—No, certainly not, but . . .

*HE.*—And of his taste for, his strange hankering after obscurity?

*I.*—Doubtless not as an aim in itself, but I approve of it when it leads to poems as luminous and glorious as Mallarmé's. He made great demands on the reader. That is what this dedication expresses in an exquisite manner:

> *Attendu qu'il y met du sien,*
> *Vous feuillets de papier frigide*
> *Exaltez-moi, musicien,*
> *Pour l'âme attentive de Gide.*[2]

---

[1] In prose: "My hunger, though regaled here by no fruits, finds equal savor in their learned absence."—Tr.

[2] This inscription for Mallarmé's young friend might read in English verse:

> Because he also does his part,
> White paper in your frigid sheets,

*HE.*—Then poetry, in your estimation, should tend toward the esoteric?

*I.*—Poetry should tend, or pretend, only to perfection. Obscurity is something that the true poet should neither seek nor fear. What he should fear is affectation. Mallarmé's obscurity has yielded to the commentators. But I did not have to wait for the explications of Royère, Thibaudet, Dr. Mondor, Emilie Noulet, or Mauron, however excellent these may be, to fall in love with his poems.

*HE.*—Does this mean that you understood them perfectly without assistance?

*I.*—No; but rather that I did not feel the need to understand them perfectly; and that their meaning, which gained rather than lost by remaining a little imprecise, mattered a great deal less than the almost religious emotion aroused in me by their mystery. Their sonorous and incantatory power was such that they preserved the strange charm of that mystery in spite of the explications I afterwards received. Lovelier verses I have never read.

That poetry, to quote the learned Florentine quattrocentist, Marsilio Ficino, might "by its very nature be filled with enigmas" is a truth that was scarcely admitted in the seventeenth and eighteenth centuries; but rest assured that Mallarmé, in his esotericism, was reviving an ancient tradition of which John Donne in England and Maurice Scève in France were illustrious

---

Inspire the musician to new feats
For André Gide's attentive heart.

Mallarmé is the musician; it is Gide as the listener who "also does his part."—Tr.

representatives. They too had made it their resolve and regarded it as a point of honor to remain *secret*. "If the words used by a writer bear within them . . . a hidden subtlety"—*acutezza recondita*, in Ficino's own expression—"they give as it were more authority to his style; they cause the reader to advance more slowly, to rise above himself, to consider more attentively what is said to him and . . . by tiring him a little, they let him taste the pleasure attached to the pursuit of difficult things." [3]

*HE.*—Yes, that is well said. But doubtless the esotericism of the Renaissance poets consisted largely in teasing the reader's mind with hidden meanings; the poems offered enigmas to which, in many cases, erudition furnished the only key; so that we should be wrong to confuse this sort of obscurity with that of Mallarmé, who aims to be incantatory, in the proper sense of the word you applied to him.

*I.*—Obviously when Scève begins one of his Dizains with the lines:

> *Le Cerf volant aux abois de l'Austruche,*
> *Hors de son giste esperdu s'envola*

—"The flying Stag, tracked down and flushed from his covert by the Ostrich, takes desperate flight"—the only allusions concealed in his verses are historical (as they are elsewhere mythological); and this is also the case in Dizain LV, where he again refers to Charles V of Spain

---

[3] These remarkable phrases were brought to the attention of French readers by M. Eugène Parturier, who quoted them in his excellent introduction to Maurice Scève's *Délie*. No longer having the book with me, I am unable to verify the quotation, but hope that I copied it correctly.—A. G.

and Austria under the guise of the *Austruche.* But, by
effort and as if incidentally, he nevertheless achieves the
same incantatory power that Mallarmé seeks and attains
directly. In Scève's case, as too often with Gérard de
Nerval, the effort is intellectual and, by that very fact,
remains foreign to what constitutes the essence of poetry.

*Amor che nella mente mi ragiona*

—"Love that torments my mind"—was, if I remember
correctly, what Dante said in one of the *Canzone* of his
*Convito.* To address oneself to the intellect is to invite
arguments. Hence all I should like to retain from Marsilio Ficino's remarks is this: that the poet should seek
in the art of verse an obstruction or at least a means of
delaying the poetic flood, a recourse against facility;
that he should charge his words with more meaning than
is granted them by current speech and, by holding back
the reader, "by tiring him a little," should permit him to
enjoy, in the midst of this very fatigue, a reward that is
not to be obtained without pains. On this point there is
much more to be said, and we shall return to the subject
if you choose. No more for today.[4]

---

[4] After this interview was published in *Le Figaro,* an obliging and
sharp-sighted correspondent informed me that the fine phrases I had
lent to Marsilio Ficino had been borrowed from Baldassare Cas-
tiglione. The absence of reference books is not an excuse to be
pleaded for another and more serious error: in this same interview I
have attributed to St. Paul words that were spoken by Christ in the
"Sacerdotal Prayer" (St. John xvii, 15), a mistake that covers me
with confusion.—A. G.

# IMAGINARY INTERVIEW · 13

*Metrics and Prosody*

THAT day my interviewer did not appear; he had written me requesting permission to send a younger friend in his place. I could hardly fail, the letter said, to welcome a poet-poet, a representative of the new cohort, "all the more representative for not being very original." But I felt that it was hardly the occasion for Virgil's *ab uno disce omnes;* the young man could not speak for his whole generation, which had the good fortune to be diverse and multicolored; what he had to say would engage nobody but himself. To leave no doubt of his being a poet-poet, he had sent before him a thin book of verse, which I had time enough to read. Blushing in an engaging fashion, he begged me to tell him frankly what I thought of it, and he blushed still more when I said in so many words that his poems were no good. What pleased me was that he did not try to defend them.

"No doubt I published them a little too soon," he said, "and wrote them too fast. Any other year I should have spent more time on them. But what can you expect?—I was hurried."

*I.*—Hurried by what?

*HE.*—By the paper shortage. I was afraid that if I waited too long, there would be no chance to print them, and I felt the need of proving my existence to myself, if not to others. Please don't smile; youth feels an impatience that is not understood by those of riper age. We run while we still have light to see. There is so little assurance for the future!

*I.*—It is true that the future of our literature depends on the future of France; but, if you please, let us confine ourselves to poetry. The indisputable but amazing fact that we are now witnessing a lyrical renaissance should swell your breast with hope. From all sides rise the songs of unsuspected poets. . . . Or are you perhaps afraid that when everybody is singing, there will be nobody to hear you sing?

*HE.*—No, don't impute such a niggling idea to me. Rivalry is a good source of inspiration. It is only when poets are singing in chorus that a new prosody can take shape. And yet I am not without anxieties and I envy the assurance of several comrades whose verse is doubtless no better than my own. Shall I confess to you what I sometimes think we are? A sacrificed generation.

He said these frightful words without any great emphasis, with a simplicity that touched me. I protested, with the kindliest air that I could assume:

*I.*—What puts that idea into your head? There was never a time when the older writers were more solicitous about those who came after them.

*HE.*—I know, I know. We are receiving only too much attention. In all senses of the word, we are being *exposed;*

and we should have more chance to ripen if we were let alone. Some of my young friends are delighted to see their poems regarded by other young friends as finished works; they too regard them as such. In reality we are all groping.

*I.*—The songs of these young poets seem to me a little hoarse, I confess, as if their voices were changing. And yet I could mention the names of several who have given us something better than mere hope for the future.

*HE.*—No doubt the names would be those of the poets who are closest to the past and remind you of former delights. Didn't you once say: "In art, what the public likes is first of all what it can recognize?"

*I.*—That is still true. But I remember three Latin words that Valéry liked to quote in the days of our youth: *Ars non stagnat*, art is not a stagnant pool. The future belongs to the innovators.

*HE.*—They have a thankless task. They are not listened to, or not understood. But no matter; there are many of us who think that nothing but plaster copies can come from the ancient molds.

At that moment he saw Auguste Dorchain's book, *The Art of Verse*, lying on my table. Indicating that he had read it, he asked me what I thought of it.

*I.*—Dorchain was undistinguished as a poet, but he was an excellent teacher. He speaks of "liberty within discipline" and "surprise within security"; one couldn't find better phrases. The examples he quotes in his book are remarkably well chosen. But when he comes to discuss lines of eleven syllables, I am surprised and disappointed to find that he doesn't mention Verlaine's admirable "Crimen Amoris," a poem that would have offered strong support to a thesis he has been advancing all through the book: that only an established rhythm and metrical pattern can explain the charm of a verse that subtly evades them. Dorchain talks very well about the past, but stops a little too soon. He does not understand Francis Jammes and he seems to suspect that any change in the position of the cesura in an alexandrine indicates that the poet lacks a delicate ear.

*HE.*—As I was reading him, I thought to myself: "Happy were the poets of a more fortunate age, who inherited from their ancestors a lyre with taut strings, one on which their whole originality could be exercised while the tuned instrument brought out its value!" Today the lyre is broken, or at least all its strings are loose; they have been pulled too often in all directions.

*I.*—On the contrary, you should have said: "Happy are the poets born in this age of a new dawn, who must tune the sonorous strings again for chords never heard before!"

*HE.*—Is there a single example of a poet who was able to invent new chords and, at the same time, to perfect them? Those whose songs we admire have profited from the discordant voices of many others, perhaps no less talented, whose energies were exhausted in seeking new harmonies. The work of every illustrious poet seems to me less a point of departure than the end of a journey.

*I.*—Is there a single example of a great poet who, after possessing himself of the past, was unable to find the new and personal expressions that accorded with his particular genius? Every future is built on what has gone before, and each of us might answer, like the watchman calling out of Seir: "The morning cometh, and also the night." At every moment something is beginning and something is ending. Young poets should be concerned with beginnings; let old men weep over what is passing and the dead bury their dead. Out of all you say, there is only one point I should like to stress: you recognize that no system of poetry can do without laws.

*HE.*—In the same way that no dance can do without an established rhythm. Yes, I know and feel that a poem must submit to external laws, but so far we haven't found the laws that will govern the poems of tomorrow. Instead of accepting artificial rules, or creating them for myself, it seems to me that what I must seek is sincerity of expression.

*I.*—All poetic rules are more or less artificial. What is not and must never become artificial is the use that the poet makes of the rules. But that is another subject. . . . Since you speak of sincerity, I hope you are not confusing it with mere unconstraint, the gush of poetic language, and with the sort of lyric facility that some poets flatter themselves by confusing with inspiration, although real art laughs at it contemptuously.

*HE.*—Not in the least. Sincerity, as I understand the word, is something difficult and intractable; it demands of us a constant seeking, a refusal ever to be satisfied, a knowledge of and a mastery over oneself that I am far from having achieved. Oh, if I simply let myself go, I confess that my verse would follow the ancient

formulas; but wishing as I do to make a new beginning,
I must forget rhymes, meters, rhythm, and cesuras. At
the same time I realize that the magic of poetry depends
on laws observed and resistance overcome. . . . Oh, no,
please don't think that facility is what I am seeking; on
the contrary, it is resistance. Given too much liberty, I
flounder. If we except Whitman, the savage, and the un-
governable Claudel, I can think of no poetic genius, however fiery, who did not submit when writing to the rules
of a strict prosody. Even Apollinaire; even Rimbaud.
You once said that the most daring artists, those who
felt an imperious need for struggle, were also those who
sought the most resistant material and the harshest limitations. I remember that you spoke of Michelangelo's
sonnets and the tense gesture of his *Moses,* which was
inspired, so we are told, by a flaw in the marble; and
Dante's *terza rima* and Beethoven's restless search, in
one of his last quartets, for the obligations of the fugue.
Today we are finding it all too easy to knead a substance
that is still soft, yielding, and inconsistent. We are working in lard.

He had spoken these last words with a sort of raging
sorrow and had taken his head in his hands.

*I.*—If your friends heard you say that—

*HE.*—Oh, please don't tell them what I said!

For some time I abandoned him to the childish despair
of which I had tried to cure him. Then at last:

*I.*—So you are interested in questions of technique?

For it had occurred to me that there is nothing like
the love of sound workmanship to restore a man's con-

fidence. My question in fact, made him start; he regained control of himself and

*HE.*—I should so much like to know what you think about rhyme.[1]

---

[1] Although the remaining pages of this dialogue are concerned with the rules that govern French verse—and they are quite different from those observed by English poets—Gide is also talking about the spirit of poetic discipline in any language whatever. Those unfamiliar with the French rules might turn to the "Note on French Prosody" printed in the Appendix.—Tr.

# IMAGINARY INTERVIEW · 14

THE young poet-poet, forgetting to be dejected, had asked me in a great burst of confidence what I thought about rhyme. I chose a roundabout way to answer him.

*I.*—No development can take place without breaking the old husks. They burst from the pressure of the new sap within; but it is from their fragments that new husks are formed, and new limitations. I confess to you that I should find it hard to do without rhymes. It is a matter of habit, perhaps. But it seems to me that some of our recent poets are all too eager to get rid of them. By suppressing rhymes, and the expectation of rhymes, they sacrifice the exquisite element of poetic joy that Dorchain discussed: surprise.

*HE.*— I should have thought, quite on the contrary, that they had banished rhyme because it had lost its capacity for surprising us. Marriages of words in which we can guess the bride from seeing the groom are already too abundant with Maurice Scève, and they spoil some of Ronsard's loftiest passages. We find two adverbs with an equal number of syllables, like *innocemment* and *incessamment;* two verbs from the same root,

(125)

like *suivre* and *poursuivre, vivre* and *revivre, brunir* and *rembrunir;* two antithetical nouns, like *presence* and *absence;* two words as closely related as the adjectives *juste* and *injuste* or the word *couche* first taken as a noun and then as a verb. I prefer the poorest weddings to these incestuous unions.

*I.*—On the other hand, think of this: that rhyme is what inspired the verbal genius of Hugo. Far from being hindered by rhyme, he made it his tool, just as on the island of Guernsey he made use of table-tipping; it launched his imagination on new ventures, opened the gates to infinite horizons; and his most admirable flights were made possible by rhymes, the more unexpected the better, which he sometimes achieved at the cost of what prodigious delays, what slackening of his pace, what detours! Far from letting his emotion seek the rhyme, he set out from the rhyme (and that was his secret) in search of an idea or of an image to take the place of an idea. Was it not the effort to give his rhymes a glorious fullness (an effort that seemed almost unconscious in his case, although with Rostand, and even earlier with Banville, it became a matter of erudite search and preciosity) that inspired him to bold, mysterious, terrifying evocations like:

> *Et verrons-nous toujours les mêmes sentinelles*
> *Monter aux mêmes tours?*

—to answer the call of the preceding verse:

> *L'homme a-t-il sur son front des clartés éternelles?* [1]

---

[1] "Brightness eternal" (in the plural) calls forth the rhyme "sen-

*HE.*—Rather I should swear it was the word "senti-nels" that occurred to him first.

*I.*—That is possible, or they both might have occurred simultaneously. And what shall we say about his fashion of using proper names, with a strange power of sugges-tion, at the ends of his verses?

> *En voyant la colline, on nommait le satyre;*
> *On connaissait Stulcas, faune de Pallantyre.*

*HE.*—

> . . . *On entendait Chysis,*
> *Sylvain du Ptyx, que l'homme appelle Janicule,*
> *Qui jouait de la flûte au fond du crépuscule.*

*I.*—But it's a pleasure to talk with you.

> *Et même la clameur du triste lac Stymphale,*
> *Partie horrible et rauque, arrivait triomphale.*

Three examples among a thousand; for we can find an abundance of everything in that great bazaar of genius.

*HE.*—Then you are for the preservation of rhyme?

*I.*—I am not for or against the preservation of any-thing whatsoever. Each poet has his own particular method of working and must find a personal answer to all the problems that face him, as well as a different answer to each problem. I admire Hugo for his lordly

---

tinels": "And shall we always see the same sentinels/Climbing the same towers?" Since the lines of verse in this interview and the one that follows are quoted for their rhythm or their rhymes, both un-translatable, I shall, in most cases, omit the English versions.—Tr.

rhymes; but I also admire La Fontaine, who rhymes in
a most offhand fashion, with a specious appearance of
being easily satisfied that allows him to devote all his
attention to the exquisite appropriateness of the phras-
ing, the tone of the dialogue, and the pace of the narra-
tive. Perhaps he also felt that rhymes beginning with
the same consonant would, by their richness, distract
the reader's attention. At any rate he didn't bother to
find them; and one feels grateful to him for not attach-
ing great importance to rhyme, so pleasing are the
effects he achieves with simple assonance. He is not
ashamed to couple *logis* with *pays* or *grands* with *dents*; [2]
in poverty of rhyme he finds the same element of surprise
that Hugo found in richness; and his tolerance in the
matter of final syllables makes it possible for him to
triple his rhymes and sometimes even quadruple them.

*HE.*—The English poets offer many examples, so I
am told, of a similar ease and negligence. A rhyme that
is too rich impresses them as being barbarous, and they
are a little disdainful of the savage pleasure it can give
the ear. And didn't Milton go so far as to banish rhymes
completely from his epics?

*I.*—Shall we read together what he says about them
in his foreword to *Paradise Lost*?

*HE.*—Alas, I don't know English.

*I.*—I'll translate as I go; listen: "*La rime n'est nulle-
ment un appoint nécessaire et l'ornement naturel des
poèmes (particulièrement ceux de longue haleine) mais*

2 Both these pairs of words would be acceptable rhymes in English,
since they end in vowel sounds that are identical. But the French are
more exacting.—Tr.

*bien l'invention d'une époque barbare. . . ."* And I continued to the end of Milton's foreword:

". . . Rhyme being no necessary adjunct or true ornament of poem or good verse, in longer works especially, but the invention of a barbarous age, to set off wretched matter and lame meter; graced indeed since by the use of some famous modern poets, carried away by custom, but much to their own vexation, hindrance, and constraint to express many things otherwise, and for the most part worse than else they would have expressed them. Not without cause therefore some both Italian and Spanish poets of prime note have rejected rhyme both in longer and shorter works, as have also long since our best English tragedies, as a thing of itself, to all judicious ears, trivial and of no true musical delight; which consists only in apt numbers, fit quantity of syllables, and the sense variously drawn out from one verse into another, not in the jingling sound of like endings, a fault avoided by the learned ancients both in poetry and in all good oratory. This neglect then of rhyme so little is to be taken for a defect, though it may seem so perhaps to vulgar readers, that it rather is to be esteemed an example set, the first in English, of ancient liberty recovered to heroic poem from the troublesome and modern bondage of rhyming."

*HE.*—So that, all things considered, you disapprove of rhyme?

*I.*—Let me repeat: I neither approve nor disapprove. Many recent poets (including some of the best) throw it overboard. They are free to do so. Simply I doubt whether French verse can do without it so easily as verse in English, German, Italian, Spanish, or any other language having stronger accents than ours. With us it comes forward to atone for the inadequacy of the meter, as Milton said in somewhat different words. And if we had learned in our classes to scan Latin and Greek verses in a fashion less abstract, theoretical, and generally absurd than pupils are taught, or at least were taught in my schooldays, we should understand better and in fact should feel instinctively why neither the Greek nor the Latin poets resorted to rhyme.

*HE.*—As Milton says, they found true musical delight "in apt numbers, fit quantity of syllables, and the sense variously drawn out from one verse into another."

*I.*—Our metrics are based on the number of syllables, with no attention paid to their length or accent; and this is especially true of our own times, since the new poets who write alexandrines with two or three cesuras, or with none at all, have come to neglect the stronger accents which, in our classical writers, preceded and emphasized the pause in the middle of the line and marked the end of each verse. Nothing puzzles foreigners more than to hear us, when reciting poems, give the same value to a mute "e" as to the full vowels. These three verses:

*Considère, Phœnix, les troubles que j'évite* . . .
*Vivez, et faites-vous un effort généreux* . . .
*Nous partîmes cinq cents, mais par un prompt renfort* . . .

would impress them as having only eleven syllables each; this other:

*Et ma gloire, plutôt digne d'être admirée*

as having only ten; while perhaps they would find only nine in:

> *Cet ennemi de Rome et cet autre vous-même.*

*HE.*—That last verse seems weak to me. What do you think of it?

*I.*—At least it is perfectly correct. So too is this ridiculous line that I invented:

> *Je ne le ferai plus, dois-je te le redire*

in spite of its eight weak syllables;[3] it is quite as correct as alexandrines that contain nothing but strong vowels (we have to look for them, because twelve-syllable verses without a mute "e" are not common):

> *Dès qu'on leur est suspect on n'est plus innocent* . . .
> *Ils sont partis pareils au bruit qui sort des lyres* . . .
> *Nous mettrons notre orgueil à chanter tes louanges.*

*HE.*—A great fuss has been made about the poetic role of the mute "e." Critics assume an air of mystery when they discuss the place it should occupy in the alexandrine.

*I.*—As you know, it was always a matter of choice. The place assigned to the mute "e" in a line of verse was deter-

---

[3] In conversation, four of the "e's" would be omitted: *"Je n' le f'rai plus, dois-j' te l' redire."* Maurice Grammont says, in his *Traité pratique de prononciation française:* "When the 'e' drops out, it is not diminished or reduced, but is suppressed completely; when it is retained, it is pronounced as distinctly as any other unaccented vowel." But, he adds: "In classic and romantic verse, all the 'e's' in the interior of a line must be fully sounded." In verse, Gide's line, however absurd, would have all its twelve syllables.—Tr.

mined by the poet's feeling for language. There has been no rule to govern it.

*HE.*—At least there were rules that decided other questions of versification. When they weren't followed, we were able to say that such and such a verse was faulty.

*I.*—And when they were followed strictly, every regular verse could be passed off as a good verse, with dangerous consequences for the art of poetry. It was dying from faithful observance of the rules. It achieved a new life by breaking those which had become obsolete, but then it subjected itself to others; it always seeks new laws; poetry cannot do without them. They evolve themselves little by little from the best poems of their time.

*HE.*—That casts light on a verse of Hugo's I never completely understood, the one where he says that without the River Styx there is no Fountain of Youth:

*Comme il n'est plus de Styx, il n'est plus de Jouvence.*

*I.*—It comes from his admirable poem on the death of Théophile Gautier. Its meaning, I always thought, was sufficiently explained by the preceding line:

*L'onde antique est tarie où l'on rajeunissait*

—"Dry are the ancient streams that washed the years away."

*HE.*—What I didn't understand was the reason why Hugo, in this verse, established a connection between Styx and Juventas, between death and rejuvenation. He must have meant that the death of old forms is a condition for the birth of new ones.

# IMAGINARY INTERVIEW · 15

MY CONVERSATION with the young poet-poet turned to questions of accentuation in French verse.

*I.*—The intonation of our language is too smooth to justify a prosody based on alternating light and heavy beats. French students of foreign poetry are puzzled as soon as it has to be scanned, not by syllables, but by metrical feet. Yielding to our own habit, we might, if you please, consider the iambic pentameters of Goethe's tragedies as ten-syllable verses; but in that case we run the risk of being disconcerted when we find that his *Elegies*, for example, contain many trisyllabic feet, anapests or dactyls, that are used as the exact equivalents of his iambs and spondees. Back in the days of Symbolism, there were a few experiments in writing verse based on French accents, weak and sometimes changeable as these are. In most cases the experiments were confined to isolated verses; the wager was too difficult to be sustained through a whole poem. I remember, among others, a verse of Henri de Régnier's which might be regarded either as having fifteen syllables or as being composed of three spondees followed by three anapests, so that it could be scanned as a sort of hexameter:

> . . . (*où le pavé des places*)
> *Vibre au soir rose et bleu d'un silence de danses*
>     *lassées.*

In those happier times, I too attempted a few verses in the same rhythm:

$$—\,—/—\,—/—\,—//\cup\cup—/\cup\cup—/\cup\cup—/\cup$$

and even finished a short poem with which I was, and still am, rather well satisfied:

> *L'air chantait sur les flots. Les ceintures de l'aube*
>     *étaient pleines.*
> *L'interminable champ s'emplissait derrière elle de*
>     *fleurs . . .*

*HE.*—Couldn't the first of your two verses also be scanned in this fashion:

$$—\,—/—\cup\cup/—//\cup\cup/—\cup\cup/—\cup\cup/—\cup$$

and the second:

$$—\cup\cup/—\cup/—//\cup\cup/—\cup\cup/—\cup\cup/—$$

*I.*—Perhaps you are right. But note the indecision from which we suffer. Can anything solid be built on these shifting sands?

*HE.*—Take a verse from Racine, for example:

> *Le jour/n'est pas/plus pur//que le fond/de mon*
>     *cœur.*

Isn't it composed of three iambs followed by two anapests? And many other verses of four anapests? For
instance:

> *J'ai conçu/pour mon cri// me une jus/te terreur.*
> *En public,/en secret,//contre vous/ déclarée?*

*I.*—Beyond a doubt; and the alternation of strong
and weak syllables gives the verse, it is true, a sort of
secret animation. All French syllables are certainly not
of equal weight. The actor in classical tragedies should
make that clear. But if he puts too much emphasis on
the accented syllables, as if he had in mind a different
pattern from that of our classical verse, the alexandrine
is dislocated and the charm is broken. There are certain
actors who seem to devote all their talent to concealing
the fact that they are speaking in verse. They make me
long for a diction that leaves or gives an approximately
equal value to each syllable.

*HE.*—Hugo sometimes amuses himself by writing
verses with heavy, unmistakable beats. You must remember this one, in which he imitates the sound of a gallop-
ing horse, and in which the three iambs of the second
hemistich take full advantage of the liberty granted by
our alexandrine:

> *Cheval! foule aux pieds l'homme, et l'homme, et*
> *l'homme, et l'homme.*

*I.*—And this other, in which the three iambs occur in
the first half of the line:

> *Il est! Il est! Il est! Il est éperdument.*

It is amusing, surprising, and even, if you wish, a mark of genius; but these verses remain exceptional and, in the following line, Hugo tames his savage prosody. He is careful to do the same after every verse in which the cesura is displaced or seems indefinite; for example, when he indicates a pause after the fifth syllable. I have noted several of these lines. Listen:

> *Le bombardement fait gronder nos citadelles.*
> (*L'Année Terrible*)

> *O beaux jours passés! terre amante, ciel époux!*
> (*Le Titan*)

> *Et dans on ne sait quel cintre démesuré.*
> (*Dieu*—"Les Voix")

*HE.*—Isn't the most typical example to be found in the piece that we all had to learn by heart in school, "After the Battle"?

> *Et que le cheval fit un écart en arrière.*

The professor never failed to make his pupils admire the fashion in which the unaccustomed pause after the fifth syllable rendered the sudden fright of the steed.

*I.*—Don't you find it remarkable that, in each of these examples, the word coming after the misplaced cesura is a monosyllable? The reader can pause slightly after pronouncing it, and thereby indicate where the normal cesura would be:

> *Ainsi vous parliez,//voix,/ grandes voix solenelles.*

Moreover, the broken verse is surrounded by others that are regular and reassuring; for Hugo bears no more grudge against prosody than he does against syntax. He uses the rules as a fixed bar on which to perform his boldest acrobatics.

*HE.*—Unless there is resistance, the mind has no base from which to rise. Yes, we began by saying that the young poets must seek new laws.

*I.*—And that poetry without restrictions is poetry without art.

*HE.*—Without art? What about Eluard? I defy any critic whatever to find a system of prosody in his poems. Yet today he has more disciples among the younger men than any other poet; and for my own part I confess that . . . Do you know what I sometimes think? That rhymes, regular meters, and cesuras are meaningless survivals from a time when they used to serve as aids to memory; from a time when poems were learned by ear. There is nothing more difficult to memorize than one of Eluard's peoms. A little while ago you were speaking of the delight caused by surprise: well, in Eluard's case, what one feels is astonishment at every phrase, every image, every word; he breaks every link, even with his subject. I smile when people tell me that they can't understand a word of his poetry; as if there were anything to understand; as if what can be explained did not cease to be Poetry, the very essence of which is inexplicable.

*I.*—Eluard disturbs me. He is like a door opening into the unknown; like a journey toward one cannot say what destination, and perhaps toward nothing at all. On the other hand, Aragon reassures me, it may be even to excess; he represents security and achievement, the journey's end. We owe him a double debt, both for having returned to rhyme and for having restored it to youth and vigor by giving it a new breadth and flexibility. No wonder that I shrug my shoulders when I hear you speaking of your "sacrificed generation."

*HE.*—So you would advise me to . . .

*I.*—I advise you! Let me tell you this: people listen to the advice of others with much less effort, and hence more willingly, than they listen to their own. But rest assured that your own advice is all that counts. And follow it. In any case you aren't going to begin rhyming just because Aragon does. If you are too undecided, if no inner force compels you or guides you, there is still another solution: you can renounce.

*HE.*—Renounce poetry? Never!

*I.*—Who spoke of that? But you can renounce verse, in favor of prose . . . or life. Bear in mind a line from Francis Jammes that I may not be quoting correctly (I have stumbled so often in my quotations):

*Jadis la poésie était dans le commerce*

—"There was a time when poetry was in trade." No doubt we have great need of lyric ardor, heroism, enthusiasm, and abnegation; but I am still to be convinced that some of our younger writers could not find a better use for their fervor than pouring it vaguely into facile poems; than courting a muse who turns away her face, a woman they cannot and will never be able to master.

Seeing that his features were clouding over, I hastened to add:

"I am not saying that for you, of course, since you are tormented by an authentic demon; but for scores of others who think themselves chosen when they have not even been called; who have never understood that Inspiration is the daughter of labor and not of laziness; and who in the future, having been disillusioned and perhaps embittered, but having learned no trade that at least could save them from poverty and render them useful, despising themselves and despised by others, will join the outcast legion of those who have failed. These are, and these will be, the sacrificed."

*HE.*—You aren't very encouraging.

*I.*—It is not wise to encourage artists. True artists, the only ones we need, are those who never let themselves be disheartened; who, as you said, treat resistance as a base from which to rise; whose energy contracts at the sight of obstacles and prepares to spring forward. These have no need of encouragement. As for the others—

*HE.*—Still I know that you have helped more than one.

*I.*—One's heart often contradicts one's reason. Then too, aiding and encouraging are not altogether the same thing. Good-by. Go back to work on your poems. Be less easily satisfied. Study the successive versions of Mallarmé and Baudelaire; you will see that their finest poems were the most carefully revised. Rest assured that it is the same for all good poets; but ordinarily the public doesn't see the changes they make.

# IMAGINARY INTERVIEW · 16

## *The New American Novelists*

I HADN'T seen my interviewer for more than a year, but at last he ran me to earth again;[1] he wanted to talk about the issue of *Fontaine* that would be devoted to American literature. In what I thought was a rather disrespectful manner, he expressed surprise at my interest in the subject, hinting that nothing in the world seemed farther from my proper field.

"I have met two sorts of people in my long career," was what I began by saying. "The first sort consists of those who fall in love with everything that resembles themselves, in literature and art as well as in nature, and who feel cheated by any work that doesn't offer their image in a mirror. The second consists of those who travel through countries or books in search of an admonitory strangeness, and who enjoy a landscape all the more for its being different from themselves. I belong to the second class. There is no contemporary litera-

---

1 This interview was written in North Africa, after Gide had been liberated from German-occupied territory by the capture of Tunis. It reached this country too late to be included in the French text of *Interviews Imaginaires.*—Tr.

ture that arouses my curiosity more than that of the United States; not even that of the new Russia."

I added that there was nothing recent about my eagerness to hear what America was saying, and that I was probably one of the first in France to admire Melville, having urged my friends to read him long before Giono undertook his translation of *Moby Dick*. It was the same with Thoreau's *Walden;* I remember the day when Fabulet met me in the Place de la Madeleine and told me about his discovery. "An extraordinary book," he said, "and one that nobody in France has heard about." It happened that I had a copy of *Walden* in my pocket.

"As regards more recent books," I continued, "other Frenchmen were ahead of me; it was Malraux who had me read Hemingway and Faulkner. I have to admit that it took me some time to become acclimated to the latter, although I now regard him as one of the most important, perhaps *the* most important, of the stars in this new constellation. It was· Steinbeck, however, who gave me the keenest satisfaction. When it comes to Dos Passos, I admire him more than he captivates me. He gives the impression of having a formula; his pointillism wears me out, even though it is highly effective; and his intrepid modernism is the sort that seems old before its time. I have trouble following him through a series of snapshots that dazzle me one after the other; they remain so unrelated in my mind that, after patiently reading the 500-odd pages of *Manhattan Transfer* or *The 42nd Parallel,* I should have been completely incapable of grouping my successive impressions around a center, and even of deciding what the author had said, about whom. Nevertheless I had been held and dominated from page to page; I was forced to admit that here was 'something big.' "

*HE.*—Might I ask whether you have read these new authors in the original?

*I.*—The truth is that I usually have to depend on translations, but several of these impress me as being first-class; those by Maurice Coindreau and Michel Tyr in particular. I have no trouble understanding English, but it seems to me that American has been tending more and more to become a separate language. Very often I find myself halted by phrases or idioms that make me wish for a new dictionary, since they aren't to be found in those we now possess.

*HE.*—That must be quite troublesome.

*I.*—Much less so than one might suppose. It might even be that the author sometimes gains by these fleeting misapprehensions, since his meaning perhaps falls short of what I imagine it to be. The difficulty of the language also keeps me from making hasty judgments. Thus I can't be sure about the accuracy of certain dialogues; in *The Grapes of Wrath*, for example—

*HE.*—That is supposed to be Steinbeck's best book.

*I.*—I should prefer *In Dubious Battle*, a novel in which the most urgent and bitterly argued of social questions is presented (I almost said "played") in a wholly impartial light, with a profound feeling for psychology and a very sure artistic sense that leads to compelling simplifications and formalizations, thus transforming this picture of a strike and all its complicated issues into something bold and legendary. But Steinbeck, in

my opinion, has written nothing more skillful and nearly
faultless than some of the stories in a volume called *The
Long Valley;* they equal or surpass the best tales of
Chekhov.

*HE.*—I hear that *Fontaine* has asked you to write
an essay on the present status of literature in the United
States.

*I.*—I feel that I am not at all qualified for the task.
Although I have read more than a score of books by
their new novelists, I know scarcely anything about their
poets. It is good to hear that our friend Jean Wahl is
presenting their work in translation.

*HE.*—Mightn't you at least make some general statement about the work of their novelists?

*I.*—Not even that. It would require more perspective,
in spite of the fact that distance in space is often equivalent to distance in time, as Racine maintained in the
preface to *Bajazet.* Some of these novels seem very far
from us, and yet—don't you agree?—they touch us
closely. Above all this is true of Hemingway, and particularly of *A Farewell to Arms,* which is so palpitating
with life and rich in a sensibility that is interfused with
intelligence. I have none of his love for bull-fighting,
and yet there is no American author I would rather meet.

*HE.*—I grant you Hemingway, since he is the most
European of them all. As for the others, I have to confess that their strangeness appals me. I thought I would
go mad with pain and horror when I read Faulkner's
*Sanctuary* and his *Light in August.* Dos Passos makes
me suffocate. I laugh, it is true, when reading Caldwell's
*Journeyman* or *God's Little Acre,* but I laugh on the

wrong side of my mouth. There is no doubt that each of
these great novelists impresses me as having a powerful
individuality; and yet, after the simple but resolute and
instinctive optimism of Whitman and Emerson and Melville, how do you explain that these more recent writers
have chosen to portray an equal depth of abject suffering and blindness? If one believes what they are saying,
the American cities and countrysides must offer a fore-
taste of hell.

*I.*—Don't believe a word of it. Each of these authors
is a realist, it is true, but in his own fashion. When he
paints the American world for us, he isn't so much reflecting as opposing it. One might say that each of them
is achieving a consciousness of his own nature by reacting. Faulkner in particular, with his Southern back-
ground, is and remains essentially, powerfully, and in
the full sense of the word a *Protestant*.

*HE.*—I remember a remark of Rathenau's that you
set down in your *Journal.* "America," he told you in
1921, "has no soul and will not deserve to have one until
it consents to plunge into the abyss of human sin and
suffering." I quote these words from memory because
they impressed me.

*I.*—Ever since the last war, American literature has
done its best to draw people out of the soulless contentment that Rathenau was talking about, not to mention
the state of quivering lethargy and mechanized innocence
that was depicted in Sinclair Lewis's *Babbitt.* Dreiser
already, the first of their somber authors—unless we
go back to Edgar Allan Poe . . .

*HE.*—Yes, these new writers have taken the great

plunge into the abyss, Faulkner especially; and yet there is not one of his characters who, properly speaking, has a soul. For them and for him the moral question simply doesn't exist.

*I.*—It doesn't exist in the new Russia either. Perhaps it doesn't exist anywhere except as a human invention. I wonder whether it hasn't tormented us long enough. Might it be that a new humanity is preparing to abolish it? . . . But that discussion would carry us too far.

*HE.*—Something else surprises me: the stubbornly and violently æsthetic, literary, and at times even artificial aspect of some of these recent productions. I was thinking, for instance, of Faulkner's extraordinary *As I Lay Dying.* Does that represent still another reaction?

*I.*—Against reporting; there isn't much doubt of it. America is the country of reporters. Now, just as photography absolved painting from reproducing nature and imitating the real world, might we not say that in America, more than anywhere else on earth, reporting carried to a state of perfection—as in Dana's masterpiece, *Two Years before the Mast*—had the effect of purging literature of everything that did not properly belong to it? I don't know, I am asking a question. We are speaking of random impressions.

And speaking at random, there is one recent author, Dashiell Hammett, who is doubtless not in the same class as the four great figures we began by discussing. Again it was Malraux who drew my attention to him; but for the last two years I have been vainly trying to find a copy of *The Glass Key,* which Malraux specially recommended; it couldn't be procured either in the original or in translation, whether on the Riviera or in North Africa. Hammett, it is true, squanders his great talent on detective stories; they are unusually good ones, no doubt, like *The Thin Man* and *The Maltese Falcon*, but a little cheap—and one could say the same of Simenon. For all of that, I regard his *Red Harvest* as a remarkable achievement, the last word in atrocity, cynicism, and horror. Dashiell Hammett's dialogues, in which every character is trying to deceive all the others and in which the truth slowly becomes visible through the haze of deception, can be compared only with the best in Hemingway. If I speak of Hammett, it is because I seldom hear his name mentioned.

*HE.*—You haven't said anything about Caldwell. Is that because you think he is less important?

*I.*—Not at all. But I haven't been drawing up a list of prize-winners for commencement day. If I haven't spoken about Erskine Caldwell, it is because he puzzles me. He evades the categories and theories that I am trying to elaborate; what I was saying about the others does not wholly apply to him, and that is all to his credit. But the quality in which he resembles them is the interest he takes in life. All these new American novelists are seized and held like children by the present moment, by the here and now; they are far from books and free from the ratiocinations, the preoccupations, the feelings of remorse that darken and complicate our old world. That is why a closer acquaintance with them can be very profitable to those of us who are burdened with the weight of our too rich past. Good-by. Leave me quickly before I start thinking of objections.

# CHARDONNE 1940 [1]

CHARDONNE's last book is revealing and calls for our careful attention. You remember the title he gave to one of his recent novels: *Love Is Much More than Love*. The title frightened me and I never went any farther. Love is already a solemn word; I feared that the "more" would be too much. Imitating his phrase, I am now tempted to say that Chardonne's last book is much more than Chardonne's last book: it is the instructive example of a disposition or, one might say, an indisposition of the intelligence. However nebulous it may be, it helps us to understand. The book seems so loosely constructed that it is hard to discuss in any systematic fashion. From

---

[1] I copy a footnote by M. Jacques Schiffrin, the editor of the French text: "Although it was written before the *Imaginary Interviews,* this chapter, which is not an 'interview,' is placed after them, so as not to disturb their unity. 'Chardonne 1940' first appeared in the April 12, 1941, issue of *Le Figaro;* it was the answer to *Chronique privée de l'An 1940,* a book that Chardonne had published in Paris a short time before. Chardonne's book was the first literary work in the French language that, from an allegedly French point of view, idealized the German victory over France. Together with a complacent acceptance of disaster, it contained a plea for the domination of Hitler and the Germanic race over Europe."—Tr.

one chapter to another there is no connecting thread,
no plot; it is not a novel but a random daybook and, as
the title indicates, a *Private Chronicle of the Year 1940*,
in which the only focus is the personality of the author;
and even that seems to be dissolving before our eyes.

"I do not demand the key to any enigma," the author
tells us, "nor assume any fixed position. The most important things that life has told me were vague, and I
thought it was better so." In the whole book we shall
find him regarding the "vague" with an attitude of vague
compliance that suggests the acceptancy of the Dukho-
bors (those apostles of the doctrine of non-resistance
to evil) or the resignation of the Brahman, while at the
same time it resembles the sort of spiritual dilettantism
that Anatole France displayed at intolerable length and
that Chardonne, in this book, carries to the point of absurdity, as if trying to outrival him in preciousness. He
excels in the game of mystic leapfrog that consists in
first depriving a word of its proper meaning (as in the
title cited above) and then vaulting over its back, but
only to face about and, a moment later, give the same
word a new meaning of his own. One example is the
phrase: "dying from not dying," which has enchanted
certain delicate souls; it grates on my nerves. "There is a
life of the soul," he says, "in which everything is clear
and necessary . . . a life of the Spirit . . ." (and it is
the author himself who uses the three dots; I am quoting
his text exactly), "more simply a life of reflection for
which the word 'disappointment,' for example, does not
exist, *nor any other word in its common meaning.*" Well,
well, that sounds promising.

The book starts with a portrait of Charles Du Bos,
in whom Chardonne, like the rest of us, admires "a delicate sense that escapes common perceptions." But Du
Bos is able to surmount his own preciosity when he comes
to deal with certain vital questions ; at such moments he
has written vigorous pages full of a deep conviction that
almost surprises us as coming from such a quintessential
spirit ; while Chardonne, for his part, goes on refining
the already refined. In the stratosphere into which he
invites us to follow him, there is no air for our lungs and
everything becomes so subtilized that it slips from our
grasp. Already, in the preceding volume of his *Chronicle*
(and later we shall come back to it) one might have read :
"My life is of today ; it consists of formless, fluid, almost
inconsistent things" ; and he says in his new book : "At
one and the same time we are rebels and loyalists, open
and secret, adapted to the community and ill-adapted,"
which is equivalent to saying that we are no matter what ;
at the same time everything and nothing at all. Or again :
"I have never attached importance to the literary tastes
of my friends, nor to my own ; nor to their political
opinions, however firmly held ; nor to their features, their
characters, or their beliefs ; nor to anything that I can
define" ; and suddenly he makes us realize the importance
that the properly French spirit attaches to *definition*,
precisely the field in which the French excel. It is not
that Chardonne hesitates, as I may have done too often,
nor that his sense of fairness holds him back while he
weighs the pros and cons ; no, he is not a puzzled man,
but a cloud-worshiper who admires the formlessness of
his thoughts for its delectable iridescence, and who lets

himself be pleasantly rocked on a sea of inconsistency;
I should choose these lines from the *Bateau ivre* as an
epigraph to his book:

> *. . . où flottaison blême*
> *Et ravie, un noyé pensif parfois descend.*[2]

"Let us distrust words that affect an air of universal-
ity; they have and conceal a very particular meaning."
The remark would seem to us more pertinent if, with
Chardonne, this sort of observation did not recur
throughout his book, answering an almost mechanical
need of his mind, which turns them out like stereotypes.
They become a nervous habit, a mania. Every *yes* hides
a *no*, and every vice a versa. Let us distrust A, for it is B.
Chardonne distrusts everything, even his own distrust
(and this time not without reason). We read: "The signs
that inspire confidence should sometimes disturb us. But
we can also be cheated by our own diffidence or distrust."
In the crucible of his mind everything is jumbled together, melted down, and turned into mingled vapors that
are lost in the wind. Thanks to all this, he achieves without pain—*non dolet*—a state of superior ataraxy.

He professes a certain irritation "at the political
opinions of the middle-class conservatives"; but lest this
statement should lead to inferences, he hastens to add:
"The opinions of the radicals are based on even lower
motives." As for his personal opinions, he doesn't cast
much light on them when he asserts: "I value only the

---

[2] From the sixth stanza of Rimbaud's "Drunken Boat." In prose:
"Where, like a pale, enraptured waterline, sometimes a drowned
and pensive corpse descends."—Tr.

political judgments of history." A little later he tells us
that, "as Schiller says, 'history judges the world' "—
which is equivalent to saying, if I understand him correctly: "Long live the accomplished fact!" Then, speaking of the historical events we have lately witnessed:
"One finds them quite obscure and in general shocking"
—and the "one" is evidently not Chardonne, for he continues: "Much later they will be explained; they will
appear natural and almost always favorable." ("I say
'almost' so as not to affirm anything that is not absolutely certain," he had written a short time before.)
Favorable to what and to whom?—the answer hardly
matters. In the suprarational and extrasensible regions
where Chardonne asphyxiates his readers, everything
ceases to be, nothing exists, everything is transformable
and equivalent; the "favorable" has merely an infinite
value.

Am I repeating myself? Not so often as Chardonne.
He says again: "The political figures tried before the
Court of Riom for the crime of irresponsibility are inno-
cent," and the statement seems clear, unmistakable; but
a moment later he adds, as if one lobe of his brain was
taking back what the other had granted: *"like all crimi-
nals"*—with a sort of innocence and unconsciousness
that, in these tragic times, might soon become criminal,
like all innocence. For him all human sorrows, anxieties,
or sufferings lose their importance: "One trembles,
weeps, or moans, but tomorrow these episodes will be forgotten. Except for physical pain, almost all our ills are
absurd." The new "almost" sets me to wondering, and I
wish he would tell us which few of the ills from which we

suffer are to be absolved and excepted from the common
absurdity. But "I wish," he says, "to regard the present
with the indifference of future ages and the wisdom of
forgetfulness." When everything is viewed from such a
towering height, the Himalayas sink back into the plain,
the present is absorbed into the timeless, into a constant
eternity, and, as he says: "Our thoughts are transposed
into serene ideas that rise above sensibility."

Chardonne quotes and approves a remark "by a mem-
ber of the British Cabinet" who was asked "in 1912 or
thereabouts: 'And now what is going to happen?'
'Nothing ever happens,' answered the witty Englishman." And yet something must surely have happened
since the summer of 1939, considering that Chardonne's
*Chronicle* for the year 1940 contains not a hint of the
tone that prevailed in his preceding volume. For instance,
the tone of sentences that it was a pleasure for me to
copy down: "A spirituality interfused with the material;
a communion of the artist with things, and the sense of
that communion, the faith it implies: all this constitutes
the French genius."

Could anything be better said? Space is lacking, and
nothing but space, for me to transcribe scores of admirable remarks that are vastly different from those he
gives us today. Why, how, in the space of a little more
than a year since he wrote his last book, has he . . . I
was searching for the right word, but I find it in a phrase
from that book: "Love, art, happiness," he said, "are
products of the alembic." Yes, that is the answer: Chardonne has let himself be alembicated. And when he de-

scribes himself at present as "a disembodied being, an inhabitant of eternity who does not see the ephemeral," how can we keep from thinking: What a painful sacrifice!

Somewhere in his earlier chronicle one reads: "In the phases of social upheavals we encounter heroes, but we no longer find artists or high morality or any attachment. Man goes to pieces in the momentary." Is that true? Is it necessary? And must we see such a remarkable mind fatally and deplorably going to pieces; must we see it so complacently accepting its own defeat? After all, something must have happened, or why should we now be forced to think, imitating once more the title of the novel I mentioned: "Chardonne is much less than Chardonne"?

Not so long ago, when he was speaking in his first chronicle about the peasants of the Limousin and some of their miserable villages, he said: "It would be better if they suffered from such deplorable housing. But they do not suffer. Always we run against the obstinacy of poor blind people content with their lot." And sadly we remember the blind contentment of Chardonne today.

"Almost always," he says, "a man affirms himself by reacting." Assuredly I feel the truth of that remark when reading his book. Like him the fruit of mixed heredities, with different voices arguing within me, as they do in him, I recognize in him a spirit akin to my own; that is why his book serves me as such a useful admonishment. When he affirms himself by non-affirmation, by reticence and abstruseness, by "the contrary might also be demonstrated," he plays the part of the drunken helot, warning me against the wine for which I too might have shown a weakness. Seeing him reel and stagger, at once I stand erect.

Those for whom, after all, "something has happened" since 1939 will find themselves plunged by Chardonne's book into a feeling of moral discomfort that is painful to bear but profitable at the same time. For, with his fondness for the "vague," he depicts it so well that he fills the rest of us with a more deliberate and energetic resolution to escape from vagueness. Thanks to his fluidity and inconsistency (if I judge by myself) we have a better sense of our own steadfastness and, thanks to all these indistinct surrenders, of our own constancy.

# THE DELIVERANCE OF TUNIS

*Pages from a Journal*

May 7

EXPLOSIONS and fires everywhere on the outskirts of the city. I counted more than twenty large fires. They are not the work of British or American planes: the Germans in flight are blowing up their munition dumps before evacuating the city. It is one way of packing their baggage. The sky is darkened by tragic palls of smoke.

Toward evening there are more and more fires. Great black clouds spread over the city. Through the incessant rumble of explosions, there is the strange, inexplicable crackling of machine guns close at hand. It starts to rain. For two days the main highways that intersect within sight of our terrace have been full of moving tanks, half-tracks, vehicles of every sort, but now they are deserted, having been emptied as if at one blow; their silence is impressive.

*May 8*

Yesterday when I was writing those lines, the Allies were already entering the city. The rumor began to spread late in the evening. This morning I was awakened at dawn by a dull, indistinct, and steady sound like that of a river in flood. I dressed quickly, and soon I saw the first Allied tanks; people were pouring out of the neighboring houses to give them a noisy welcome. It was still hard to understand that what we had been waiting for all these months had happened at last; that *they* were *here;* we scarcely dared to believe it. What, without any more resistance, skirmishing, or pitched battles? . . . It's all over, they are here. But we were still more stupefied to learn from the first of our liberators whom we had a chance to question that these tanks and gun-carriers and soldiers belonged to the Eighth Army, the one we thought had been checked south of Zaghouan: the glorious army that had marched from the Egyptian frontier, after having swept through Libya, Tripolitania, broken the Mareth Line and the line of the Wadi Akarit, and whose progress in the south of Tunisia we had followed from day to day. How did it happen that they were the first?—by what road had they come? It seemed almost a miracle. We had imagined the deliverance of Tunis and the entry of the Allied troops in many fashions, but not in this one. In haste I closed my bag, my suitcase, and prepared to go back to the avenue Roustan; there was no longer any reason to stay in hiding. This morning all the hunted men of yesterday are emerging from the shadows. They embrace; they laugh and weep with joy. This quarter of the city, near the nursery gardens, was thought to be inhabited almost exclusively by Italians, but now there are French flags at all the windows. Quickly, before leaving my shelter, I shave off the beard that has been growing for four weeks; then, with my companions in captivity, I go out into the streets, where they haven't been seen for exactly six months. We make our way into the delirious city.

A curious fact: in this city where all languages were spoken, today one hears nothing but French. The Italians are silent or keep out of sight and only a few Arabs can be seen. In the proclamation by General Giraud that is being posted on all the walls, there is one ambiguous but menacing sentence that fills them with foreboding; their consciences are not clear: can they be the objects of this vague threat? [1] It could hardly be said that they stay in hiding, but they take no part in the celebration; they say nothing and keep to themselves in the Arab city. As a result, the cheering crowd that swarms in the streets is composed largely (and in some quarters almost exclusively) of Jews. Everybody is shouting: *"Vive la France!"* As soon as a gun-carrier comes to a stop, it is surrounded and besieged by a horde of people; children clamber over it and take their seats beside the victors. And, as if the skies had assented, all of yesterday's clouds have disappeared; the weather is superb.

---

[1] "As for those who supported the enemy in his work of spreading poverty and suffering, they will be promptly and pitilessly punished. This is my formal promise. There is no place among us for traitors." —A.G.

*May 10*

No chance to take notes yesterday. I hurried here and there, went to see my friends, mingled with the crowd. By evening I was tired out; and moreover there was no electric current, the Germans having blown up the power station before leaving the city, so that I had no light to read by and went to bed in the last glow of twilight. The sky was empty of clouds. A succession of radiant days, the finest I can remember, the finest there could be; and nights more innumerably constellated than ever before. But the city remains under martial law and nobody is allowed in the streets after eight in the evening.

After the Eighth Army, the First appeared in the city, together with French troops, Zouaves. It seems that the Eighth outdistanced the First; having circled to the north from Enfidaville (after leaving part of its force as a screen before Zaghouan to deceive the enemy), it had profited from the breach at Mateur, which had been opened painfully, valiantly, and at great cost by French infantry and American armor. All that will be recorded later, and it is not my task to set down what belongs to history.

The Germans were surprised by the suddenness of the final advance. They were evicted suddenly and without warning; their orders were to leave without taking anything except what was strictly necessary and, before going, to destroy everything that might be useful to the new tenants, as well as their own papers and personal belongings. There was a desperate flight toward Cape

Bon, but many had their retreat cut off, so that the number of prisoners was considerable; so too was the number of those who died fighting rather than surrender. A desperate stand was attempted at Hammam-Lif; all during the morning of the 8th we heard the rumble of artillery, and then this last islet of resistance melted away under the bombardment.

Yesterday the whole victorious army was drunk. On all sides there were little improvised bars where unscrupulous dealers sold out their last stocks of adulterated wines and liquors, the Germans having made away with all honest beverages. Late in the afternoon trucks began passing; they gathered up and carried back to their units all those who couldn't walk. When victory touches earth, she soils her wings.

What a marvelous day! A sort of ethereal joy floats in the air. One takes deep breaths. The daily ration of bread has just been increased from 200 to 500 grams for each person. Milk has reappeared on the market. As people are looking forward to abundant supplies and as the restrictions are being lifted, they take their reserves out of the cupboards, they open their tinned food, they dare to eat their fill. Packages of American and English cigarettes are raining down, and bars of excellent chocolate. Every meal becomes a feast. What a pity that, with the current still dead, we can't turn on our radios and listen to the communiqués from Berlin, Rome, and Vichy! Just how will they announce this appalling defeat? The official bulletins of the day before the evacuation of Tunis still maintained a confident and hopeful tone; at most they referred to "a few operations of local significance." I managed to get hold of the *Tunis Journal* for May 7, only a few copies of which were printed before the presses shut down. There I read: "Several attacks of the Anglo-Americans against the north and central sectors [*sic*] were repulsed, announces the communiqué from Berlin." Will they again seek to minimize their defeat, or will they proclaim a national mourning as after the surrender of Stalingrad? [2] In any case, this reconquest of the whole African coast will demoralize the Germans. With their strength already undermined by the Russian victories, they have doubtless begun to foresee the collapse of their hopes.

I keep as a cherished possession a stillborn issue of *Die Oase: Feldzeitung der deutschen Truppen in Afrika*, dated May 9.

*May 13*

A radiant day. . . . I sleep next to the French window of my bedroom, which leads to a narrow balcony, and let it stand wide open on a field of stars; going to bed very early, I rise at dawn. My rest is a little troubled by mosquitoes.

Day before yesterday the Ragus had me to dinner,

---

[2] Germany was clever enough to pass this defeat off as a victory. "We couldn't hope for more," her spokesmen said, "and we knew from the beginning that we should be forced to yield to superior numbers. But whereas we had counted on one month of resistance, we held out for six, thereby exceeding all our hopes. The Allies are boasting, but we are the ones who deserve to be congratulated." —A.G.

with Mme Sparrow, Hope, and two English officers she brought with her, both charming; it is a pleasure to set down their names as a memento: Captains Chadburne and Gidal, the latter being staff photographer of the Eighth Army. With both men I enjoyed a perfect understanding, in two languages, regarding all the literary matters on which we touched. Gidal spoke with great perspicacity of Stefan George, saying that he greatly preferred Rilke and giving excellent reasons for his choice. The names of Kafka, Steinbeck, Faulkner, Aldous Huxley, and others came up for discussion.

The American staff car that took us home, a little before midnight, stopped just before reaching the crossroads where, on the 7th, the first British tanks had broken the last German resistance. The road was blocked by an interminable procession of trucks and half-tracks filled with German prisoners being taken back from Hammam-Lif, where there had been a sanguinary battle the day before, followed by the surrender of the Axis troops. We stepped out of our car to watch this fantastic parade, and Gidal, with his flashlight bulbs, photographed one group of these vehicles: the prison vans captured from the Germans. It was a case of the trapper's being trapped. I was told that some groups of prisoners had been singing. Why not? To be captured was their only hope of escaping this nightmare and of seeing their families again. Others wept, so I heard. I had believed that many more would have killed themselves or have died fighting, in obedience to orders. The whole Italian army had surrendered almost immediately; and that surprised nobody. The German troops, with their supplies running short, seeing no possibility of being reinforced and no possibility of retreat by land or escape by sea, standing hopelessly with their backs to the shore, at last made up their minds to surrender; in the absence of Rommel himself, von Arnim was made a prisoner.

Speaking from Berlin or Rome, the radio announcers can save appearances by telling us that the Axis armies fought to the last man and the last cartridge, in a final heroic resistance. With that story they can try to safeguard honor and patriotic pride, but it will not be true. "Unconditional surrender," however surprising the fact may be, was almost immediately accepted. The fierce struggle at Hammam-Lif was the last pitched battle; after that, vain resistance came to an end and von Arnim announced that he would surrender.

But above all, let nothing I say here be taken as a disparaging comment on the value of the German troops. Until these last days they displayed an extraordinary endurance, discipline, and courage; they yielded only to superiority in weapons and numbers—and also, doubtless, in the final days, to the suddenness of the Allied advance, which transformed their retreat into a rout. It was only natural that von Arnim, seeing that the game was irrevocably lost, should try to avoid what would have been an inevitable and profitless massacre. My own remarks are directed only against the camouflaged story that will be carried over the Axis radios.

The African campaign, which was to have been triumphal and triumphant, ends with an enormous loss of men and munitions by the Axis. Confidence in the Führer will doubtless be greatly shaken, not to mention the Führer's confidence in himself. On the other hand, all the conquered peoples under the German yoke will find great encouragement to resistance in this immense defeat of the oppressor. It may well be the first sign of a general collapse.

Ragu tried to convince me that I had an important role to play here in North Africa and that I was the only one able to assume it. I think he is mistaken both about myself and about the influence my voice might have. Even if I were less tired, I should not feel myself in any way qualified for political action, whatever it might be. For one thing, I haven't a clear enough picture of the dissensions that are now coming to light; for another, I am too uncertain in my own mind to propose any sort of equitable middle course, and I could not speak without betraying or distorting my ideas. I cannot take part nor do I wish to get entangled in the struggle that can be foreseen. I fear that France, or at least the liberated part of France, will be divided for a long time by bitter rivalries. I fail to see what "declaration" I could make which, if it remained sincere, would not be of a nature to offend all parties.

*May 14*

From all sides we hear that the American troops fought admirably, quite as well as did the British and the French. The delays for which they were blamed in the early days were only measures of prudence dictated by their lack of supplies. It was important not to open the battle until they were assured of power enough to carry it through to a victorious conclusion. The result was such as to dissipate any remaining doubts and it showed the wisdom of this willingness to wait, at a time when hasty action would have involved the risk of defeat.

# APPENDIX

## 1. Ten Desert-Island Novels

THE list of ten French novels that Gide would take along to a desert island—if he had to go, and if he had to take novels, which have never been his favorite reading—appears in an untranslated volume of his essays, *Incidences* (1924). It begins with Stendhal's *The Charterhouse of Parma,* which he chose after balancing it carefully against *The Red and the Black.* Then comes *Dangerous Acquaintances,* by Choderlos de Laclos. "After these two novels," Gide says, "if my choice were not restricted to France, I should mention only foreign writers. . . . France is a country of moralists, of incomparable artists, of composers and architects and orators. What foreigners could be mentioned as the equals of Montaigne or Pascal or Molière or Bossuet or Racine?" On the other hand, he continues: "What is Lesage beside a Fielding or a Cervantes? What is Abbé Prévost in comparison with a Defoe?—or even, what is Balzac as measured against Dostoyevsky?" Then, having offered this warning, Gide gives the rest of his list, with explanatory comments. Some of the novels he mentions are little known in English:

3. *La Princesse de Clèves,* by Mme de Lafayette (1678)

4. *Le Roman Bourgeois,* by Antoine Furetière (1666)

5. *Manon Lescaut,* by Abbé Prévost (1731)

6. *Dominique,* by Eugène Fromentin (1863)

7. *La Cousine Bette,* by Honoré de Balzac (1847)

8. *Madame Bovary,* by Gustave Flaubert (1857)

9. *Germinal,* by Emile Zola (1885)

10. *Marianne,* by Pierre de Marivaux (1731–41)

*Germinal* was included after unfavorable comments on its style; Gide thought that "it should have been written in Volapuk." *Marianne* is a very long novel that he was taking along because he hadn't and—to judge by his failure to mention it in his *Journal*—still hasn't read it; he wanted something unfamiliar in his baggage.

---

## 2. *A Footnote on French Prosody*

THE laws that govern the writing and reading of French verse are among the most notable survivals into our own era of institutions developed in an earlier stage of society. Spoken French has been changing, perhaps more rapidly than any other language of western Europe. Written French has been changing too, as anyone can see by comparing Malraux's style (not to mention Céline's) with that of any novelist before the First World War; or better still by comparing the dialogues in this volume with the first two "imaginary interviews" that

Gide wrote in 1905 and reprinted in his *Nouveaux Prétextes*. Meanwhile the rules of prosody have remained the same, at least until very recent years. Codified by Malherbe in the early seventeenth century; enforced by the great example of Racine; strengthened by all the generations of poets who observed them in essentials, even while arguing vehemently for minor reforms; kept fresh in the public ear by the traditional diction of the French stage, they have persisted into this age of mass revolts and political religions, carrying with them the formal atmosphere and even some intonations of the court at Versailles.

In the beginning, however, the rules of French prosody were based on the specific nature of French as a language spoken at the time. Unlike Latin, it never had a system for determining which syllables were short and which were long; therefore French verse could not depend on anything resembling the Latin quantities. The language did have accented syllables, but the stresses were comparatively weak, and it is doubtful whether they have grown much stronger with the years. They fall on the last syllable of a word or group of words expressing a simple idea: for example, the French say "ma*tin*" if the word stands alone, but "matin se*rein*" and "matin serein de la *gloi*re" if it occurs in a group. The trouble is that French speakers disagree on what constitutes a group of words; in the last phrase I quoted, most of them, but not all, or not at all times, would place a secondary accent on "se*rein*." There is enough uncertainty, in any case, so that it would be difficult to write French verse based on a regular pattern of accented and unaccented syllables. The experiment was made by some of the Symbolist poets, as Gide mentions in his dialogue on "Metrics and Prosody," but it was never continued through a poem of any length.

Since French verse could not depend on definite quantities or regular accents, it was reduced from early times to the simplest possible system of measurement: it counted the syllables in a line. Each of them had an equal value, no matter whether it was light or heavy, short or long. Today, however, the syllables are not always the same as they would be in prose. The prose rule has come to be that an "e" without a mark of accent is not pronounced unless it has been preceded by two or more consonants in succession: thus, one says "un(e) petit(e), pronouncing the second of the three "e's" because it is preceded by "np," but dropping the two others. In poetry, however, the mute "e" is counted as a syllable (and is pronounced by the careful reader) unless it precedes another vowel or falls at the end of the line. "Some readers," says Maurice Grammont, in his *Traité pratique de prononciation française,* "yielding to habits learned from prose and ordinary speech, suppress some of the 'e's.' It is a mistake; they forget that the diction of verse is archaic and artificial, that the fundamental principle on which it is based is the number of syllables, and that to omit an 'e' is to suppress a syllable and make a faulty verse."

Besides this full value assigned to the mute "e," there are many other customs by which the language of poetry is set apart: for example, consonants at the ends of words are often sounded in verse where they would be

silent in conversation. The poet—unless he is a rebel—
never uses a word ending with a vowel (except the mute
"e") before another word beginning with a vowel: thus,
he doesn't say *j'ai à aller* or even *j'ai été*, to mention two
of the commonest French expressions. Two vowels coming together form what is called a "hiatus," and this is
conventionally supposed to be ugly, although in speech
it has a rather pleasing sound.

Lines of French poetry can be of almost any length
desired. In Laforgue they often consist of two syllables;
in Louis Aragon's last book, *Les Yeux d'Elsa*, there are
lines of twenty-four that are perfectly regular (unlike
Paul Fort's fifty-syllable verses). Most lines have an even
number—eight, ten, or twelve—but Verlaine preferred
the *impair* and wrote verses of seven, nine, and eleven
syllables. The one general rule is that a pattern should be
established in the first stanza and followed throughout
the poem. But in French poetry as a whole, twelve-
syllable verses, known as alexandrines, are the prevailing
measure. It was the one that Corneille, Racine, Hugo,
Baudelaire and most of the other great poets since the
sixteenth century have adopted by preference. At least
two thirds of the lines quoted by Gide in this volume are
alexandrines.

Two other features of French verse that help to com-
pensate for its lack of strong rhythm are definitely
placed cesuras and heavy rhymes. In English the cesura,
or pause within the line, can occur after any syllable,
even the first or the ninth of a ten-syllable verse. In
French it has a fixed position. The cesura of an alexandrine is supposed always to follow the sixth syllable and

thus to divide the line into two equal parts, each known as a hemistich. Since the last syllable before a cesura receives a stronger accent, the general effect is to impose a metrical pattern. The Romantic poets tried to change that pattern. In the course of their attacks on it, they succeeded in budging the cesura, but they didn't really shift its position.

Unlike English, the French language is rich in rhyming words; so rich, in fact, that a medieval poet named Pierre du Corbian wrote 840 successive lines with the same sound (it was *ens*). But lest this liberty of rhyme might lead to laxness, French poets since Malherbe have restricted themselves by obeying a whole series of more or less arbitrary rules. For example, masculine rhymes (those ending with a consonant or sounded vowel) must alternate with feminine rhymes (ending with a mute "e"). This is a rule that appeals to the eye, but in most cases not to the ear, since there is no more difference between the pronunciation of *mer* and *mère*—to mention one instance among thousands—than there is in English between "stair" and "stare." Another rule for which there is still less justification is that words ending in a consonant, even if it is silent, cannot be coupled with words that end in a vowel: thus, *doux* and *d'où* form an illicit pair, in spite of their having exactly the same sound. Often spelling seems to be regarded as more important than pronunciation. *Vénus* is an acceptable rhyme for *venus*, although the "s" is sounded in one word and silent in the other. "These distinctions," says the Grand Larousse, "may appear somewhat subtle; nevertheless our best poets have accepted them."

The strongest of our English rhymes would be classified in French as "sufficient" (or passable), while many of the others in standard use would be dismissed as either "poor" or "defective." The French prefer what they call "rich" rhymes. In English we call such combinations "perfect" or "identical" and, curiously, we have a rule against using them: thus we don't rhyme "vain" with "vein" or even, unless we are careless, "bay" with "disobey." But the French couple *regarde* with *hagarde*, *roseaux* with *oiseaux* and *chante* with *méchante*, to mention three examples from Mallarmé's "L'Azur." Of the eighteen rhymes in that poem, fifteen are "rich" and only three "sufficient." In general the use of "rich" rhymes is regarded as a mark of finished workmanship.

As time goes on, the traditional laws of French verse are coming to appear more and more "archaic and artificial," in Maurice Grammont's phrase. The separation between poetic and popular speech seems almost as sharp to a foreigner as that between colloquial Chinese and Mandarin; and one sometimes wonders whether it didn't serve as the basis for the Symbolist distinction between Art and Life. That distinction is becoming harder to maintain at a time when French poets are directly involved in life. There is some question whether the old laws of verse can survive a general disaster like the French defeat in 1940, which brought everything into question. Long before that time, the folk poets were omitting mute "e's" in reckoning the length of their verses. Learned poets, in the midst of social chaos and a lyric revival, are busy constructing new prosodies—for at all costs they must have rules; and Aragon recently developed (and

wrote a book of poems partly to illustrate) a completely
new system of rhyme that uses the actual sounds of words
but disregards their spelling. It may be that rules based
on current and changing speech may gain general acceptance. Or again, the situation might come to resemble
that in the later Roman Empire, when classical poems
and hymns in Vulgar Latin were being written simultaneously.—M. C.

### A NOTE ON THE TYPE

*This book was set on the Linotype in Scotch, a type-face that has been in continuous service for more than one hundred years. It is usually considered that the style of "modern face" followed in our present-day cuttings of Scotch was developed in the foundry of Alexander Wilson and Sons of Glasgow early in the nineteenth century. The new Wilson patterns were made to meet the requirements of the new fashion in printing that had been set going at the beginning of the century by the "modern" types of Didot in France and of Bodoni in Italy. It is to be observed that the modern in these matters is a modernity of A.D. 1800, not of today. The "modernist" type-faces of today are quite another story.*

*The book was composed, printed, and bound by H. Wolff, New York. The typographic scheme and the binding and jacket designs are by Warren Chappell.*